'WHY DO I DRINK CHAMPAGNE FOR BREAKFAST? DOESN'T EVERYONE?'

NOËL COWARD

IN FONDEST MEMORY OF MY OLD MAN,
WHOSE FAULT IT WAS I GOT HOOKED ON
FIZZ IN THE FIRST PLACE.

JONATHAN
RAY

DRINK MORE FIZZ!

100 of the world's greatest
champagnes and sparkling wines
to drink with abandon

quadrille

CONTENTS

Wines are arranged in alphabetical order, and when a wine name consists of a first name and surname, the order is dictated by the surname. The denominations 'Cave de', 'Domaine (de)', 'Castello' etc. are ignored for the purposes of alphabetization.

LUXEMBOURG: Bernard-Massard Cuvée de L'Écusson Brut NV

ENGLAND: Ambriel English Reserve Demi-Sec NV

CANADA: Inniskillin Sparkling Icewine Vidal 201

FRANCE: Le Grand Seuil NV

MASSACHUSETTS: Westport Rivers Blanc de Noirs Brut 2007

SPAIN: Codorníu Cuvée Barcelona Brut NV

CORSICA: Muscadellu Muscat Pétillant NV

WASHINGTON STATE: Domaine Ste Michelle Brut NV

CALIFORNIA: Domaine Carneros Brut 2011

ITALY: Bottega Gold Prosecco NV

SICILY: Il Grillo di Santa Tresa Vino Spumante Biologico Brut NV

BRAZIL: Miolo Millésime Espumante Brut 2012

CHILE: Miguel Torres Santa Digna Estelado Rosé Brut NV

ARGENTINA: Chandon Rosé NV

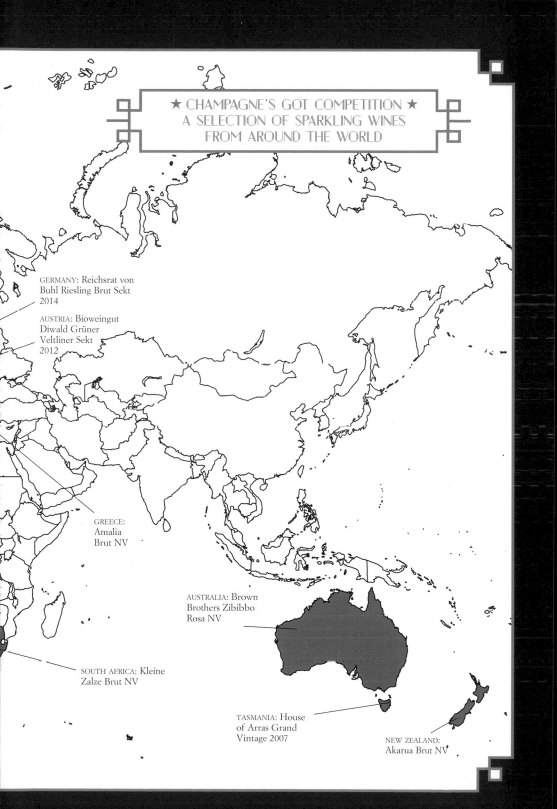

★ CHAMPAGNE'S GOT COMPETITION ★
A SELECTION OF SPARKLING WINES
FROM AROUND THE WORLD

GERMANY: Reichsrat von Buhl Riesling Brut Sekt 2014

AUSTRIA: Bioweingut Diwald Grüner Veltliner Sekt 2012

GREECE: Amalia Brut NV

AUSTRALIA: Brown Brothers Zibibbo Rosa NV

SOUTH AFRICA: Kleine Zalze Brut NV

TASMANIA: House of Arras Grand Vintage 2007

NEW ZEALAND: Akarua Brut NV

INTRODUCTION

BEING SOMETHING OF A LUSH, I HAVE A NUMBER OF FAVOURITE DRINKS THAT I TURN TO REGULARLY WHEN I NEED A BIT OF A LIFT.

Pour me an ice-cold manzanilla or fino sherry, say, a gin and tonic, a bone-dry Martini, a caipirinha, a Negroni, a creamy draught Guinness, a buttery white Burgundy, a supple New Zealand Pinot Noir or – ooh, yes please! – a luscious Alsace Gewurztraminer *vendange tardive* and I will guzzle it and come back crawling on my knees begging for more.

It's a sad, stark truth, though, that none of these delicious beverages, excellent though they all are, will raise my spirits quite the way that a cold glass of top-quality champagne or even tip-top sparkling wine will. There's just something indefinably spot-on and uplifting about fine fizz. As that great hunting man, John Jorrocks, so memorably put it in R. S. Surtees's *Jorrocks' Jaunts and Jollities*, 'Champagne gives one werry gentlemanly ideas.' No celebration, no triumph, no defeat, no birthday, no rite of passage, no seduction, no wedding, no anniversary, no kiss and make up, no gathering and no solitary moment of introspection should pass by without a bottle of fizz, bubbles, bubbly, pop, poo, champers – call it what you will – being broached.

Champagne, of course, is the acme of such fizzes and, even though the finest sparkling wines are fabulous (and the best – many of which you will meet in these pages – really are fabulous), they just don't quite have that something, that élan, that dash, that glamour, that *je ne sais quoi* that first-rate champagne possesses. And that's largely because they don't boast that magical name.

After all, would you rather go to a champagne bar or a sparkling wine bar? Live a champagne lifestyle or a sparkling wine lifestyle? Have a champagne breakfast or a sparkling wine breakfast? Be a champagne Charlie or a sparkling wine Charlie? And, well, while being a champagne socialist is one thing (and I should know: my father was an out-and-proud one), is there any point in being a sparkling wine socialist?

That being said, we shouldn't be snobs. There's no question that it's better to drink fine sparkling wine than poor champagne. And, sadly, there *are* poor champagnes out there that just don't quite measure up, being sharp, acidic, lean, green and deeply unsatisfying.

Unfortunately, we need to be on our guard against such disappointments and bear in mind that the word 'champagne' on a bottle's label is no promise of quality. All it guarantees is that the wine is made in the region of that name, using one or all of the three major permitted grape varieties (Chardonnay, Pinot Noir and Pinot Meunier) and is produced by the so-called champagne or traditional method, with its secondary fermentation in bottle.

Find a producer or producers you like – ones who use the first pressing of top-quality grapes from top sites in top vineyards and who age the resulting wines longer than the official requirement – and stick to them like glue. Ignore the makers of fizzy dross. Anyway, phooey: this book ain't about them.

Champagne might only account for 0.4 per cent of the world's total vineyard area (and just 4 per cent of France's) but with its 16,000 growers and 320 champagne houses producing 350 million bottles a year, it represents a respectable 13 per cent of the world's sparkling wine. And I'm delighted to say that in the UK we drink more of it than anybody else, bar the French. I've never been more proud to be British.

There was a time when the best champagne was the same price as the finest red Bordeaux or Burgundy. These days, it's a fraction of the cost. When I last looked, 1998 Château Lafite-Rothschild was £800 (US$1,000) a bottle. The 1998 Dom Pérignon P2 featured in this book is £250 (US$330), and the regular 1998 Dom Pérignon (if there is such a thing as regular DP) is a comparatively meagre £150 (US$200). And which would you rather have: twelve bottles of 2008 Château Lynch-Bages or eighteen bottles of 2008 Pol Roger?

And just think of the work that goes into making champagne. Hand-picked grapes from hundreds of different vineyard plots are fermented into wine with each plot kept separate; these wines are then carefully and laboriously blended, bottled, fermented again, 'riddled', aged on the lees for months (if not years), disgorged and readied for sale. And don't forget that your non-vintage Veuve Clicquot or vintage Ruinart is ready to drink the second you buy it. The Champenois do all the work for you.

The Bordelais, on the other hand, will grab your hard-earned do-re-mi before they've even bothered to bottle their wines and, once you finally get your hands on the bottles many months later, you're going to have to cellar them for several years (often at quite some expense) before they even approach drinkability. If you think of it like this, champagne is cheap.

I do accept, though, that on some occasions champagne can be inappropriately ostentatious. And, despite being well-priced for what it is, champagne can also be far too expensive for whatever you have in mind. So, for such times when it's either too flash or too expensive (or just not good enough), well, that's where the other sparkling wines come in. And, happily, there are thousands of wonderful examples around the world such as Prosecco (of course), Asti Spumante, South African Cap Classique, Cava (if you must), Californian, Australian and New Zealand sparklers, English fizz and Franciacorta (although the last two are often as pricey as equivalent-quality champagne these days). There are even bubbles from Argentina, Chile and Brazil.

Champagne would be *de trop* in the pub on the way home, whereas a Prosecco or Aperol spritz would hit the spot just so. An unfussy Roederer Quartet from California could well make a better sundowner than a more complex Louis Roederer Brut Premier from Champagne. And why crack open the chic, pricey Veuve Clicquot for your neighbours when you've got some easy-going, won't break the bank Lindauer from New Zealand and in decent enough quantity, too?

The following pages include one hundred spectacular wines from all over the world, although I would hate you to think of it as a definitive list of the world's finest fizzes. I mean, I hope it goes without saying that all of them are delicious – I wouldn't have included them if they weren't – but I would never dare claim that they were the best that could possibly be found (although some unquestionably are). No, they are merely my one hundred favourites, encountered during my thirty-year fascination with fizz, initially during my long-ago stint in the wine trade with Berry Bros & Rudd, and subsequently as a journalist, during my unsteady, wine-soaked travels around the world's great wine regions, first as wine editor of the *Daily Telegraph*, then of *GQ* and latterly as wine columnist for *The Field* and *Spear's* and drinks editor of the *Spectator*.

Some are cheap and cheerful (they start at just £8/US$10 a bottle) and some are eye-wateringly expensive (they go up to £695/US$900 a bottle – *ouch!*). Some are obvious choices, some are less so and some are downright obscure and quirky. Each one, though, is equally special in its own way, each one has a story to tell and each one has been enjoyed by me on more than one suitably effervescent occasion.

Oh, and I really should add that they're only my favourite fizzes *at the moment*. If I were to write this book next year, next month or even next week, I've no doubt at all that the selection would be different. I'm embarrassed to say that I'm ridiculously fickle and my head is all-too-easily turned. Besides, new vintages, new blends, even new wineries and new regions are cropping up all the time. Dammit, there's just so much fizz out there to enjoy!

I'm acutely aware, too, that these hundred wines reveal all too clearly my own prejudices and bias. For example, there are doubtless many more English sparklers in these pages than some folk (especially French folk) will think there should be. But, goodness, they're so tasty these days and I love them so much that I had the devil's own job whittling them down to just eight. I could easily have included several more. Ditto Franciacorta, to which I'm a relatively new but completely devoted convert. Again, I agonized for ages over which ones to include and which ones to leave out.

On the other hand, I'm afraid there are also far fewer Cavas than you are probably expecting. The thing is, apart from the very honourable exceptions I've included and which I've often enjoyed, it dawned on me as I collated my top one hundred fizzes that I just don't like Cava very much; at least, not as much as I like the other sparklers in this book. Sorry, Cava-lovers, but there it is. Please don't be cross with me and please don't write and tell me what an ignoramus I am. I get quite enough of that at home, thanks.

Anyway, there are some truly fabulous fizzes frothing away in the following pages waiting to meet you – all of them available in the UK – and I do hope you will seek them out and try them, especially if they're new to you. After all, we should all drink more fizz.

Cheers!

JONATHAN RAY
Brighton, 2017

100 WINES

THERE ARE 100 FABULOUS FIZZES FEATURED IN THE FOLLOWING PAGES, EACH ONE A WINE THAT I HAVE GREATLY ENJOYED, BE IT AT HOME, OUT ON THE RAZZLE WITH FRIENDS OR ON MY TRAVELS ABROAD.

One third of the selection comes from Champagne, the rest comes from all over the world. Nearly half of the bottles are cheap – certainly less than you would pay for a basic bottle of wine in a restaurant (one diamond). Another large portion of the wines are in the middle category – ideal for special celebrations, for which even a case won't break the bank (two diamonds). To really appreciate this drink divine with discerning company, splash out on one of the wines that fall in the highest price bracket (three diamonds). Finally, there's a bottle of Armand de Brignac, which is such an utterly decadent treat that it deserves a category all of its own.

◆ ◆ ◆ FRUGAL FIZZ

◆ ◆ ◆ MORE BANG FOR YOUR BUCK

◆ ◆ ◆ THE DRINK DIVINE

 FOR GOLDEN WEDDING ANNIVERSARIES AND LOTTERY WINS

DOMAINE ACHARD-VINCENT
CLAIRETTE DE DIE TRADITION NV

RHÔNE VALLEY, FRANCE

This little gem is a real curio and typical of the vinous oddities that my old mate, wine merchant Jason Yapp digs up on his wine-buying travels. I've been with him on a number of his trips and I invariably come back exhausted.

Jason is famous for the quirky and little-known but exquisite wines he digs up on his French forays. He reckons that it's vital to get a bit of local colour and that to understand native, little-known wines, you have to understand the folk who make them. On our last trip together this need to immerse ourselves in the indigenous vibe saw us take in a rugby match in Biarritz (with all the post-match beer that entailed), a bullfight in Dax (where we breakfasted with the *vignerons* on magnums of chilled rosé and steaming dishes of *tête de veau*), and a transvestite nightclub in Avignon, for reasons that now escape me, surrounded by burly French truckers in summer frocks discussing compressed-air braking systems and the perils of the Paris *périphérique*. By the end, I was liverish and knackered. I mean, how much local colour does one need?

But this wine is the fruit of just such a trip, albeit from the southeast rather than the southwest of France. Made in the foothills of the French Alps by the ancient *méthode dioise*, whereby a combination of chilling and slow filtration keep enough yeast cells alive to provoke a delayed fermentation, the wine then rests for at least four months in bottle before being disgorged to ensure that fermentation is complete.

A blend of Muscat (mainly) and Clairette, it's gently effervescent, with a fine, frothy mousse with tiny bubbles and a deliciously creamy texture. It's sweet and grapey on the palate and, at only 7%vol, is just right for steadying the nerves after a day in Jason's company, or for knocking back as an easy-going daytime pick-me-up. You could drink it for breakfast if blended with freshly squeezed orange juice, and, since it's both organic and biodynamic to boot, it's practically a health drink.

WWW.DOMAINE-ACHARD-VINCENT.COM

AKARUA BRUT NV

CENTRAL OTAGO, NEW ZEALAND

If you want something light, elegant, refreshing and
apéritif-like and something that speaks of New Zealand,
then this fizz is for you.

I adore the Land of the Long White Cloud and I don't
know anyone who has been there who doesn't. Much more
importantly, I adore the wines of New Zealand. Again I mean,
come off it: who doesn't? There's something for everyone: the
inimitable Sauvignon Blancs of Marlborough; the silky Pinot
Noirs of Martinborough and Central Otago; the Bordeaux
blends and Syrahs of Hawke's Bay, and the Rieslings and
Gewurztraminers of Nelson and Gisborne.

I'm happy to say there are also some increasingly fine fizzes
such as this one. It's remarkable to think that, not even fifty
years ago, all that the Kiwis produced was bland, soapy
Müller-Thurgau, planted around Auckland by the German and
Dalmatian Yugoslav settlers who had come to dig for kauri
gum on the North Island. This vino really wasn't much cop
and was known to one and all as 'Dally Diesel'.

This traditional method sparkler comes from Central Otago
where there are fewer than 2,000 hectares under vine and
where warm days and cool nights give great concentration
of flavour and excellent acidity levels. It's nigh on perfect
for growing Pinot Noir, especially in the subregion of
Bannockburn, acknowledged to be the sweetest of sweet spots.

Sir Clifford Skeggs (a former mayor of Dunedin) planted
the Akarua vineyards here in 1996, and the estate is now run
by his son, David, with Andrew Keenleyside at the helm as
winemaker. I gather, too, that fizz wizard Dr Tony Jordan
(sometime CEO of Cape Mentelle, Cloudy Bay and Green
Point) had a hand in making this.

As befits a wine from Bannockburn, it's blended mainly from
Pinot Noir (around 70 per cent) with 30 per cent Chardonnay,
and is light, delicate, creamy and easy-going – an apéritif wine
for sure – and as appealing as the *Celmisia semicordata* (New
Zealand alpine daisy to you and me) that grows on the snow
line of the rugged Bannockburn mountains, where Akarua has
its vines and which serves as the estate's logo and emblem.

WWW.AKARUA.COM

AMALIA BRUT NV

PELOPONNESE, GREECE

I have to admit that Greece is rarely my first port of call when it comes to picking a bottle on a restaurant wine list or in a wine shop. In fact – rather unfairly – it's pretty much my last port of call. But if you're in Greece itself, then what the heck do you do? Well, you have to take a bit of a punt and trust to luck.

So it was in the Trilogia restaurant in Kassiopi, Corfu, with my oldest mate, Andrew Ross, our wives and other chums. Ross knows oodles about wine and spends a lot of time in Corfu, so he should have been in charge, but he insisted on lobbing me the wine list and telling me to get a wiggle on because everyone was thirsty.

We all fancied fizz, so that's where I headed. I remember that there was an Asti, a Prosecco and a dozen or so champagnes, including Cristal, Bollinger RD and Dom Pérignon at wince-making prices. And there, tucked away in the small print, was one solitary sparkler from Greece: Amalia Brut NV from the Peloponnese. I'd never heard of it and nor had I ever heard of the grape variety it was made from: Moschofilero.

Turns out we hit the jackpot. Not only was it the same price as the Prosecco, it was half the price of the next fizz up on the list – the inevitable Moët & Chandon – and a third of the price of the one after that, the Veuve Clicquot Yellow Label. It was also unexpectedly tasty, with an aroma of freshly cut roses and citrus fruit and plenty of honey, followed by toast and ripe pineapple and peaches in the mouth. We promptly ordered two more bottles.

I later discovered that Amalia is regarded as the finest fizz in all Greece and I've since drunk it with great pleasure many times. Don't do as I did and wait until you go on your holidays to drink it; track down a bottle back home and enjoy.

WWW.TSELEPOS.GR

AMBRIEL ENGLISH RESERVE DEMI-SEC NV

WEST SUSSEX, ENGLAND

We all have a wine – maybe two or three wines – that immediately leads to a smile creeping across our chops whenever we encounter it. For me, Ambriel's English Reserve Demi-Sec is just such a wine. I simply love it. I can even feel the first twitch of a grin as I write this and I've not even had a drop yet, more's the pity.

Ambriel is the brand name given to the wines grown and made at Redfold Vineyards in Nutbourne, West Sussex, barely a cork's pop from the much bigger and better-known (but certainly no better) Nyetimber.

The 9.5 hectares of vines were planted in 2008 by Charles and Wendy Outhwaite, whose day jobs as a corporate financier (Charles) and a leading barrister (Wendy, a QC no less) helped finance the enterprise. The vineyard nestles in a glorious spot blessed with striking views across to Chanctonbury Ring and the South Downs. In winter, Ouessant sheep (the world's smallest) graze between the vines and the hedges are trimmed by Golden Guernsey goats. There's a wildlife oasis, wild and untamed, in the middle of the vineyard and no insecticides are ever used.

There are five Ambriel wines: the Classic Cuvée, the Blanc de Noirs, the English Rosé, the aforementioned English Reserve Demi-Sec and the recently released 2010 Blanc de Blancs. Only fruit grown on the estate is used, and production currently runs at around 60,000 bottles a year.

I love them all, but I love the English Reserve the most. Made from 100 per cent Pinot Noir with a dosage of some 29 grams of sugar per litre, it's a classic demi-sec – that's to say a sweet fizz that's not so sweet that one can't enjoy it on its own as a well chilled pick-me-up on a warm summer mid-morning, and not so dry that it can't match all manner of rich starters, punchy cheeses or fine desserts.

It's wonderful stuff, and if you know of a finer partner to that quintessentially English combination of strawberries and cream, pray lead me to it.

WWW.AMBRIELSPARKLING.COM

HOUSE OF ARRAS
GRAND VINTAGE 2007

TASMANIA, AUSTRALIA

When it comes to Australian fizz, this is about as good as it gets. I've certainly never had better. I've been to Oz a number of times and to New Zealand even more often. Sadly, though, I've never made it to Tasmania. I plan to rectify this as soon as I can since I pine to go, not least to see where this strikingly fine wine is made and to shake winemaker Ed Carr warmly by the hand, pat him on the back and congratulate him. It's a top-notch wine and no mistake.

The thing that strikes you at first sip is the gorgeous length and complexity of the wine plus its easy-going maturity. It has spent a full eight years on the lees, far longer than is usual – even in champagne – and then a further three years in bottle.

Ed Carr learned his trade making fizz for Hardys (whose owner, Accolade Wines, also owns the House of Arras), and in Tasmania he has found the perfect climate and terroir for first-rate fizz. Long, sunny days are followed by cold, ocean-influenced nights: ideal for the slow, gentle ripening of top-quality grapes

It's just one of those rare, unexpected sweet spots for wine just as, for example, the Hemel-en-Aarde Valley in South Africa is spot-on for Pinot Noir and Chardonnay, and the Gimblett Gravels in Hawke's Bay, New Zealand, is perfect for Rhône-like reds and Bordeaux-style blends. It's a happy quirk of nature and shows that there's life beyond the so-called Old World.

The wine is a blend of 78 per cent Chardonnay and 22 per cent Pinot Noir and fair bursts with multilayered flavours: there's honeycomb, fresh and candied citrus, mango, toast, mushroom and herbs. And each glass delivers something different. What a wine!

WWW.HOUSEOFARRAS.AU

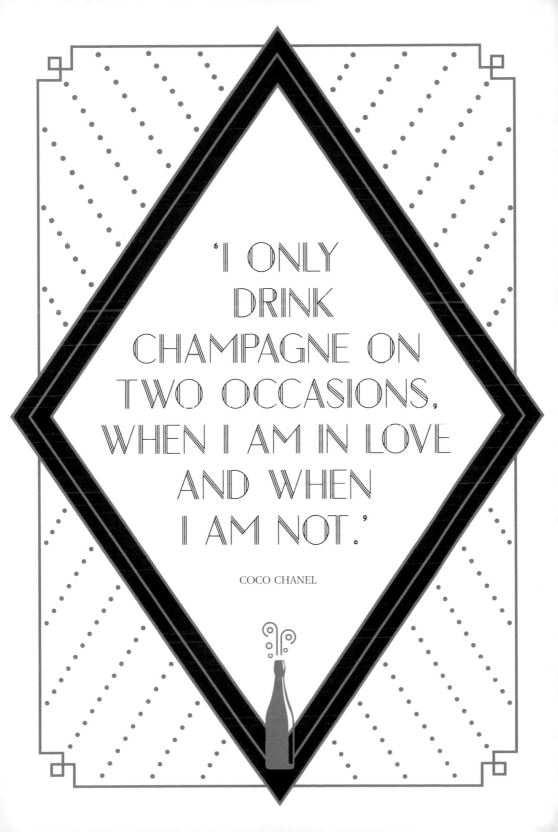

'I ONLY DRINK CHAMPAGNE ON TWO OCCASIONS, WHEN I AM IN LOVE AND WHEN I AM NOT.'

COCO CHANEL

AYALA BRUT NATURE NV

CHAMPAGNE, FRANCE

Bob Bob Ricard, in London's Soho, is one of my favourite restaurants. I spend a silly amount of time there when I should be working. BBR is Russian-owned, and no expense has been spared with the David Collins-designed décor. Indeed, it's rather like dining in a devilishly decadent Orient Express (albeit a stationary one), with each table cocooned in its own elegant private booth.

The food is excellent, a sort of modern Russian/English fusion with some classic comfort food thrown in ('Who's having the chicken Kiev? And the beef Wellington?'). The service is warm and efficient and the wine list extensive and uncharacteristically fairly priced.

Best of all, each table has a button that says 'Press for champagne'. Now that's exactly the sort of button I like to have within constant and easy reach. And clearly I'm not alone, for Bob Bob Ricard claims to pour more champagne than any other restaurant in the UK.

The brand they pour most of is the extremely toothsome Ayala, sister house to the mighty Bollinger. I don't reckon Ayala gets the recognition it deserves. This might be because it's largely an on-trade rather than an off-trade brand, or it might be because the brand was seriously in the doldrums in the 1990s.

Founded in 1860 (it's one of the original *grandes marques*), the house of Ayala is a small one, employing just fifteen people. Having been bought by the Bollinger group in 2005, it has happily rediscovered its mojo and is right back on form.

In its heyday, during the early nineteenth century, Ayala pioneered a style of champagne that was drier than usual; it's no surprise that, today, the Ayala Brut Nature, the driest style of all, is as good as it is. A blend of 40 per cent Chardonnay, 40 per cent Pinot Noir and 20 per cent Pinot Meunier, aged for four years on the lees, it has no added sugar (dosage) at all and where some non-dosage champagnes can be lean and acidic, this is just gloriously tasty. It's pure, clean and refreshing, with plenty of citrus and white stone fruit and an ever-so-slightly savoury finish: You won't find a better example.

WWW.CHAMPAGNE-AYALA.FR

WAYS TO MAKE WINE FIZZY

Just as there are several ways to put a spring into your step (drinking champagne being one of them), so there are several ways to put bubbles into wine. The best way – the most complicated, the most expensive, the most time-consuming, the most important and the most revered – is the so-called traditional method/*méthode traditionelle* or champagne method/*méthode champenoise*. This is the way that all champagnes are made, as well as many English sparklers, Cavas, Franciacortas, crémants and top New World fizz. Basically, it's the daddy of all methods.

Grapes are pressed and the juice fermented, usually in stainless-steel tanks but sometimes in oak barrels. The resulting wines, which will probably have come from different grapes, different vineyards, different plots and – in some cases – different vintages, are then blended together and bottled under a crown cap, with the addition of a wine/yeast/sugar solution known as the *liqueur de tirage*. This solution encourages a second fermentation to take place in the bottle, thus creating the precious bubbles.

The bottles are left to mature on their sides for a minimum period that varies from region to region but which in Champagne is an officially sanctioned twelve months for non-vintage fizz and three years for vintage. In practice, however, it's usually much longer than this, especially for vintage champagne and especially when being made by top producers.

The bottles are then 'riddled' (the *remuage*): that's to say that they're twisted and turned regularly, usually by mechanical means. Some very few producers still do this by hand, gradually tilting the bottles so that the lees (the sediment or gunk left behind from the fermentation) falls to the head of each. The neck of each bottle is then frozen and the icy plug is shot out of the bottle by removing the crown cap in the *dégorgement* or disgorgement. The bottle is then topped up with a dosage of wine and sugar (the *liqueur d'expédition*), which will determine the ultimate dryness or sweetness of the wine. The bottle will then rest for an officially controlled minimum period before release. *Et voilà*: you have champagne!

The transfer method is similar to the traditional method in that the secondary fermentation takes place in bottle. It differs in that once the wine has spent time on its lees after fermentation, it's transferred to a pressurized tank where it's filtered, adjusted with the dosage and then bottled. It's a cheaper and quicker method (no riddling) than the way they make champagne, and you should be aware that when a label states that a wine is bottle-fermented, it will have been made by this method rather than the traditional method. You can bet your favourite ice bucket that the wine won't be quite as complex or profound.

Prosecco is one of many wines made in a very different way, using the so-called Charmat method, also known as the tank method or *cuve close*. Here, the wine undergoes its secondary fermentation in a sealed, pressurized stainless-steel tank rather than in bottle, the sugar and yeast being added to encourage said fermentation. It's bottled under pressure and is cheaper and quicker than the traditional method, so it is particularly suited to producing light, fresh and undemanding wines.

The cheapest of all fizzes are produced simply by adding carbon dioxide as you would add CO_2 to water to make soda water. It's simply known as carbonation, or what the French jokingly like to call the *pompe bicyclette* method, and produces wine that might be as cheap as chips but isn't nearly so tasty.

BANFI ROSA REGALE
BRACHETTO D'ACQUI 2015

PIEDMONT, ITALY

This extremely tasty curiosity comes from Piedmont, northwest Italy, and I'm not sure that I know of any other wine quite like it, although its nearest equivalent would be Lambrusco. It's made by Banfi, a name well known to lovers of fine Brunello di Montalcino.

John and Harry Mariani, two Italian-American brothers who owned Banfi Vintners in New York City, fulfilled their long-held dreams of owning a wine estate in Italy by founding Castello Banfi in Tuscany in 1978. It's here that they made their Brunellos, doing much to improve the image of the local wines and helping make them the sought-after success they are today.

A year later the brothers bought Bruzzone, a century-old winery near Strevi, in Piedmont, with a view to making white wines from grapes such as Cortese and Moscato and red wines from such as Albarossa, Barbera, Brachetto and Dolcetto. Today the company is run by the brothers' children: first cousins James Mariani and Cristina Mariani-May.

Made from 100 per cent Brachetto grown in a single vineyard known as 'La Rosa' near the town of Acqui Termi, this ruby-red sparkler is light, fresh, lively and really quite seductive. It's barely 7%vol and is delicately rather than unctuously sweet. It's redolent of rose petals, strawberries and raspberries and completely disarming. It's perfect with summery fruit desserts, or on its own just for the heck of it.

I've never come across any wine made from Brachetto outside Piedmont, and folk say the wine made here is the direct descendent of *vinum acquense* (wine of the Acqui) – the wine said to be an aphrodisiac, which Julius Caesar and Mark Antony gave Cleopatra during their respective attempts at flinging woo. But look where it got them.

WWW.CASTELLOBANFI.COM

GRAHAM BECK BRUT ROSÉ NV

WESTERN CAPE, SOUTH AFRICA

English sparkling winemakers might still be agonizing about what term to give their wines – if they give them any (see page 126); they can't even agree on whether they should or shouldn't. But the South Africans have nailed their colours firmly to the mast. Any wine made in the traditional method in South Africa is termed Méthode Cap Classique or MCC for short.

There are certain quality standards that producers have to stick to, such as the minimum aging period on the lees before disgorgement (nine months), but there is no restriction as to which grapes to use (Chardonnay, Pinot Noir, Sauvignon Blanc and Chenin Blanc are the most popular), nor where MCC might be made. After all, South Africa is a big place, with around 100,000 hectares under vine in 27 specific Wine of Origin areas, all of which are very different geographically and climatically.

It might sound a mouthful, but if you walk into any bar or restaurant in Cape Town and find yourself fancying some fizz, you'll be surprised how natural it is to ask 'Could I have a chilled glass of Cap Classique, please?' and how pleased you will be by the results, especially if it's a Cap Classique made by the legendary Pieter 'Bubbles' Ferreira, head winemaker at Graham Beck.

There are three levels in the Graham Beck range: the Non Vintage Collection; the Vintage Collection and the Prestige Collection. The Graham Beck Brut Rosé NV is from the first, entry-level range and is the perfect place to start. A blend of Pinot Noir and Chardonnay drawn from vineyards in Robertson and Stellenbosch, it's so lightly coloured that the weight and complexity on the palate come as some surprise. There are hints of crushed raspberries, wild strawberries and fresh herbs in the glass and it's backed by a long, dry finish.

There's no question that it's a wonderful wine, and Pieter Ferreira more than deserves his reputation as South Africa's finest sparkling winemaker.

WWW.GRAHAMBECKWINES.CO.ZA

BELLAVISTA FRANCIACORTA NECTAR NV

FRANCIACORTA, ITALY

Prosecco has famously taken the world by storm. And the best examples are very good indeed: light, zesty, fruity and disarmingly undemanding and approachable. Who doesn't crave a well-chilled Prosecco at the end of the working day? Or – even better – a well-chilled Bellini or Aperol spritz, in which Prosecco is the crucial ingredient?

Delicious, though, the best Proseccos are (and the best are wonderful, just as the worst are pretty grim), they can't hold a candle to Italy's least well known but finest fizz by far: Franciacorta. This glorious wine, produced along the southern banks of Lake Iseo in Lombardy, between Bergamo and Brescia, is a much more complex and intriguing wine than Prosecco. It's *il bel paese*'s gift to the world – well, its gift to the world along with Monica Bellucci, Gioachino Rossini, *Cinema Paradiso* and pesto alla Genovese.

Bellavista was the first Franciacorta I ever tried, and it was a complete revelation. It quite took me aback, for I had no idea that sparkling wines outside Champagne – especially sparkling wines from Italy, best known for said Prosecco and Asti – could be so stylish, so sophisticated, so elegant and so – well, damn tasty.

I've returned to the winery twice now to taste the entire range, and on closer acquaintance Bellavista continues to impress. Made from 100 per cent Chardonnay, produced in the traditional method, this example is its rarest offering, being deliberately sweet with a dosage of 38 grams of sugar per litre, highlighting rather than masking the wine's exquisite character and making it the perfect partner to rich starters, cheeses and desserts.

WWW.BELLAVISTAWINE.IT

FRATELLI BERLUCCHI
CASA DELLE COLONNE ZERO
FRANCIACORTA RISERVA 2008

FRANCIACORTA, ITALY

Although Franciacorta producers look to champagne (both the wine and the region) for inspiration, they don't want to imitate it. They are Italian and make Italian wine. They are as different from the French as mozzarella and olive oil are different from foie gras and butter.

The soil is similar to that of Champagne, yes, but crucially the climate is warmer. This gives ripeness. Cooling breezes off Lake Iseo and the surrounding mountains add freshness and perfume, and the grapes boast higher natural sugar and lower acidity than those of Champagne, meaning that less sugar needs to be added to the wines. Indeed, most Franciacortas such as this one are *pas dosé*: that's to say with no added sugar at all, so ripe is the fruit.

And where Prosecco is made by the cheap so-called Charmat or tank method, Franciacorta is made using the finer and more laborious traditional method, with its vital secondary fermentation taking place inside the bottle. Little wonder, then, that Tilli Rizzo of Fratelli Berlucchi, one of the region's finest producers, declares that Franciacorta is the Fiat to Prosecco's Ferrari, the private jet to Prosecco's Budget Air.

The Berlucchi family started making still wine in Franciacorta in 1927 and sparkling wine in 1973. Continuity is everything, and their head winemaker has been here for 45 years, proudly producing clean, pure, food-friendly wines.

This example made from 70 per cent Chardonnay and 30 per cent Pinot Nero has no residual sugar at all. But whereas all too many so-called brut zero or zero dosage champagnes are sharp, acidic and teeth-judderingly dry, this is gloriously palatable, with plenty of natural ripe fruit at the core and a long, persistent citrusy, biscuity finish.

WWW.FRATELLIBERLUCCHI.IT

BERNARD-MASSARD
CUVÉE DE L'ÉCUSSON BRUT NV

GREVENMACHER, LUXEMBOURG

I've only been to Luxembourg once and it rained non-stop, despite being the height of summer. I might just as well have stayed in England.

It just so happened that I had arrived, completely unplanned, on the eve of Luxembourg's National Day – Grand Duke Henri's official birthday – and despite the driving rain, the city was fully en fête, with stalls, stages and pop-up bars on every street and in every square.

I dumped my bags in the hotel and went for a wander. I stopped under a dripping parasol and, in an effort to restore my flagging spirits, ordered a glass of crémant, the Luxembourgish sparkling wine that everyone drinks. And, blow me, it was utterly, completely, overwhelmingly delicious! Why had nobody told me that Luxembourg crémant – made in the traditional method – was so good? Creamy, toasty, fruity and zesty, it was better than many a champagne I've had. And, as I later discovered, Luxembourg's Alsace-like still wines are equally knock-backable.

The brand I drank most during the course of the long weekend was Bernard-Massard, and I was so taken with it that I made a special detour to visit the family-owned winery in Grevenmacher, slap-dab on the banks of the Moselle River and the Luxembourg/German border. I hadn't realized what a big business it was, producing some 3.5 million bottles a year.

I tasted several of the range, but the one I kept coming back to was the Cuvée de l'Écusson Brut NV. It's an absolute delight, launched in 1971 to celebrate the fiftieth anniversary of the winery and now a regular on the list. As I say, it's made in the traditional method, but from a slightly different blend than you would find in champagne: namely Chardonnay (40 per cent), Pinot Blanc (35 per cent), Pinot Noir (15 per cent) and Riesling (10 per cent) and it's wonderfully elegant, with buttery, creamy fruit and a fine acidity.

And, bizarrely, given that everything else in Luxembourg seems to be eye-wateringly expensive, it's very well priced.

WWW.BERNARD-MASSARD.LU

BERRY BROS & RUDD
CRÉMANT DE LIMOUX NV
BY ANTECH

LANGUEDOC, FRANCE

My former employer, Berry Bros & Rudd, recently revamped its range of own-label wines to whoops and cries of delight from wine-lovers and critics alike. When I worked there almost twenty years ago we had barely half-a-dozen such wines, the most notable of which was the inimitable Good Ordinary Claret, still to this day the company's runaway bestseller. The House Red and House White were pretty decent too, now I think about it, and I remember we found that a bottle of each made excellent wickets for our shop-based cricket matches when things were quiet.

I also remember my boss (and current chairman), Simon Berry, explaining that any fool could source, market and sell a bottle of 1982 Château Lafite, but that it took real skill to do the same with an own-label wine. This had to be pitch-perfect in terms of both quality and price, and couldn't rely on simply being a famous name.

These days Berrys' has over fifty own-label wines and each one's a corker. I recently persuaded them to offer a small selection of the wines to our readers at the *Spectator* and this peach of a fizz was top of the pops, going down an absolute storm.

A Crémant de Limoux from the Languedoc, it's produced by one of the region's largest and longest-established producers, Antech Limoux, still family-owned and run. A blend of Chardonnay (mainly), Mauzac and Chenin Blanc, it's produced in cahoots with Berrys' by Françoise Antech, the sixth generation of her family to make wine. It's made in the traditional method and is crisp yet creamy and is beautifully rounded and delicately honeyed. There's plenty of lively ripe fruit, too, and I wasn't surprised at all that it went down so well with *Spectator* readers.

WWW.BBR.COM | WWW.ANTECH-LIMOUX.COM

Champagne

sourire de la France

BILLECART-SALMON
BLANC DE BLANCS GRAND CRU NV

CHAMPAGNE, FRANCE

Billecart-Salmon is one of those fabulous fizzes that seems to slip under many people's radar. It always surprises me that, despite being so well known and admired by its devotees, so many champagne-loving folk I come across claim never to have heard of Billecart-Salmon. And those who have heard of it seldom think to buy it or order it in a restaurant.

More fool them, because Billecart is one heck of a fine fizz. Founded 200 years ago by brothers-in-law Nicolas-Francois Billecart and Louis Salmon in Mareuil-sur-Ay (the same small village that's home to the very fine Philipponnat Champagne), the house remains in the hands of the same family today, run by brothers Francois and Antoine Roland-Billecart.

I've always enjoyed the family's champagnes. They're stylish while also being understated. Maybe it's that understatement that makes the Billecart-Salmon brand such a chic one.

I remember sitting in the cigar 'sampling lounge' at the Bulgari Hotel in London's Knightsbridge a year back with the impossibly urbane Eddie Sahakian of Davidoff. The room was full of beautiful, well-heeled folk whom Eddie and I were happy to watch glide by while we puffed on our Cohiba Selección Reserva Media Coronas, a chilled bottle of 1999 Billecart-Salmon between us. I remember thinking, as I sank into my leather armchair, *Life doesn't get much better than this.*

A couple of hours later I was back home, reeking of cigars and alcohol, batting away such uxorial questions as 'Where the bloody hell have you been?' and 'What time do you call this, you moron?' Be that as it may. The Billecart had done its trick and for a brief shining moment I led the good life.

But although that 1999 Billecart-Salmon was a peach, it's this Blanc de Blancs Brut that I admire most. A blend of 100 per cent Chardonnay harvested from four *grands crus* villages in the Côtes des Blancs (Avize, Cramant, Chouilly and Le Mesnil-sur-Oger, just so you know), it's fresh, elegant and stylish, with hints of almonds, apple, zesty citrus and a touches of dried fruits and brioche. A class act in every way.

WWW.CHAMPAGNE-BILLECART.COM

BISOL CREDE PROSECCO VALDOBBIADENE BRUT 2015

VENETO/FRIULI, ITALY

I first came across this perfect Prosecco in the Hotel Danieli in Venice, an establishment way beyond my station. Don't be daft; I wasn't staying there. I simply needed a pee, having just walked the length of the Riva degli Schiavoni. While there, though, I thought it would be foolish not to take advantage of the hotel's fabled Bar Dandolo.

Parading my ignorance, I asked head barman Robert Naccari for a Bellini, that sublime drink made from Prosecco and peach juice, and was politely but firmly rebuffed. He pointed out that it wasn't the season for white peaches, and since they only used fresh juice at the Danieli, natch, I would have to come back between May and October. Or go to Harry's Bar, where he believed they used frozen juice. Ouch.

Signore Naccari steered me gently towards a Bucintoro instead. Sometimes known as a JoJo, this turned out to be Prosecco and fresh strawberry juice and utterly delightful. I remember knocking one back very happily before moving on to an equally delicious Puccini (Prosecco and mandarin orange juice).

I felt every inch the local, until Signore Naccari pointed out that locals wouldn't be seen dead drinking such cocktails. They would either have an Aperol spritz or Prosecco on its own. I chose the latter path and was completely charmed. Bisol has been the Danieli's only brand of Prosecco for more than 35 years and it proved to be light, delicate and full of apples and honeysuckle. Prosecco is often thought of as the poor man's champagne, but I felt anything but deprived as I sipped at my gently frothing glass and watched the glitterati stroll by.

Some months later I met Gianluca Bisol himself, the fifth generation of his family to make Prosecco. He explained that it was a mistake to compare his wines with champagne. As he pointed out, although they are both sparklers, they are so different: made from different grape varieties and by different methods. 'Since there is no question in my mind that champagne is the king of the bubbles,' he said, 'I like to think of Prosecco as the prince.'

WWW.BISOL.IT

'I DRINK IT WHEN I'M HAPPY AND
WHEN I'M SAD. SOMETIMES I
DRINK IT WHEN I'M ALONE. WHEN
I HAVE COMPANY I CONSIDER IT
OBLIGATORY. I TRIFLE WITH IT IF
I'M NOT HUNGRY AND DRINK IT
WHEN I AM. OTHERWISE, I NEVER
TOUCH IT - UNLESS I'M THIRSTY.'

LILY BOLLINGER

BOLLINGER SPECIAL CUVÉE BRUT NV

CHAMPAGNE, FRANCE

I was weaned on Bollinger. Well, pretty much so. It was certainly the first champagne I ever tasted, and a bottle of Bolly always marked the memorable events at home; birthdays, anniversaries, triumphs and failures. My father wrote what I like to think of as the definitive book on Bollinger and he made no bones about the fact that it was his favourite fizz of all.

He had me knocking it back more or less as soon as I was able to knock back anything, not least because he didn't have much truck with non-alcoholic drinks. I was on watered-down red wine by the age of eleven. 'What on earth do you want to drink milk for?' he once asked me when I was very small. 'You're not a calf! For heaven's sake, boy, it's what they make umbrella handles out of.' And once, remonstrating with me for drinking Coca-Cola, I replied that it was delicious and how would he know anyway, because he'd never tried it? Of course he'd tried it, he said. 'In 1936, the same year I tried cornflakes.'

It was alcohol all the way with my father – fine fizz especially. And no fizz, according to him, was finer than Bollinger. How right he was! It's my favourite, too. Well, equal favourite with Pol Roger. Bol and Pol: I love them both and I can't choose between them.

The Bollinger Special Cuvée is just so classy. Forget that it's the champagne of *Absolutely Fabulous* and the James Bond films; just luxuriate in its quality. By the way, Bolly is the only champagne to feature in the 007 films since its first appearance in *Moonraker* in 1979 – the deal done on a handshake between Christian Bizot, then head of Bollinger, and Cubby Broccoli, with no money ever changing hands.

The house was founded in 1829 and remains family-owned. It is one of the last houses to ferment any of its wines in oak and some of this finds its way into the Special Cuvée, the resulting complexity being one of the house's hallmarks. Another is the dominance of Pinot Noir, which forms 60 per cent of the blend.

Bollinger is a class act in every way and whenever I see a bottle I just know that everything is going to be OK.

WWW.CHAMPAGNE-BOLLINGER.COM

BOTTEGA GOLD PROSECCO NV

VENETO/FRIULI, ITALY

Longer ago than either of us cares to admit, I took my beloved to Venice, plied her with a brace of Bellinis on the terrace of the Gritti Palace Hotel overlooking the Grand Canal, and by the time we had reached Harry's Bar for dinner, we were – much to our mutual astonishment – engaged. It's amazing what one can achieve with just a couple of fizzy drinks and dash of Venetian moonlight.

I remember Sandro Bottega's response when I told him this tale. 'We Italians adore pretty girls,' he said, 'and we find that Prosecco, which we also adore, is the most useful of methods in getting to know them.'

Well, if you can't make any progress in that direction with a bottle of Bottega Gold – Sandro Bottega's brainchild – then you're not really trying. It's a marvellous example of this most Italian of wines, the top of the Bottega range. Not only does it come in a striking gold bottle (rather over-the-top, bling-wise, you might think), it tastes pretty damn fine, too.

Made from 100 per cent Glera (the grape formerly known as Prosecco), it's the palest straw-yellow in colour, with a very fine, persistent mousse. It's lightly aromatic on the nose, with flavours of pears and baked apples and the faintest touch of honey.

Bottega makes some 500,000 cases of Prosecco each year. The fruit is grown in the absurdly steep vineyards that lie in the foothills of the Dolomites, in the Province of Treviso, between the small towns of Valdobbiadene and Conegliano.

The rules governing production have changed recently, and to qualify for the finest *Denominazione di Origine Controllata e Garantita*, or DOCG, status, the wine must not only come from this officially sanctioned area, but must also be made from at least 85 per cent Glera, the balance being made up with such grapes as Chardonnay and Pinot Bianco and little-known indigenous varieties Bianchetta, Perera and Verdiso.

Enjoy this golden beauty well chilled on its own, or as a seductive Bellini or JoJo. But be careful as to where and when you drink it and with whom.

WWW.BOTTEGAGOLD.COM

BREAKY BOTTOM SPARKLING BRUT SEYVAL BLANC 2010

EAST SUSSEX, ENGLAND

Breaky Bottom is a glorious spot, its own secret kingdom, set in an achingly pretty fold of the South Downs at the end of an all but impassable mile-long farm track near Lewes. And king of all he surveys is winemaker-proprietor Peter Hall; his queen is wife Christina.

Peter – now 74 – first came here as a general farm worker in his early twenties. He lived in Brighton and commuted each day to the farm. One day the boss asked him to head over the hill to Breaky Bottom to fetch some sheep. It was a barren spot in those days, with no trees to speak of. There was just a simple farm cottage with no amenities, a flint barn built in 1827, and 12 hectares of rolling pasture. Peter was completely smitten.

Three years' hard graft later and Peter was the tenant of Breaky Bottom. Now the owner, he's just celebrated his fiftieth year here. He started with pigs and sheep and, in 1974, planted his first vines at a time when there were barely a dozen vineyards in the UK.

Peter started with every Loire grape variety he could think of, but none ripened satisfactorily. Eventually, he found that the hybrid Seyval Blanc worked perfectly and, despite planting a small amount of Chardonnay and Pinot Noir in 2002 and 2004, he has stuck with it as Breaky Bottom's principal variety ever since.

The 2010 Seyval Blanc Sparkling Brut was released in 2014 and promptly won the gold medal at the International Wine Challenge. It's both creamy and toasty, with perfectly judged acidity and deliciously rounded fruit.

Peter is aware that Chardonnay and Pinot Noir work brilliantly for other local wine producers and that Seyval Blanc is often sneered upon by the purists, but since anyone who tries his wine is completely seduced by it, and since he sells every bottle he produces, he's happy.

Besides, Peter reckons that there's plenty of room for variety. 'After all,' he says, 'just because French girls are pretty, it doesn't mean that English ones aren't.'

WWW.BREAKYBOTTOM.CO.UK

BENJAMIN BRIDGE BRUT 2011

NOVA SCOTIA, CANADA

Toronto is one of my favourite cities. Not because it's beautiful (it isn't, in my view) but because of its fantastic restaurants and bars. I don't think I've eaten and drunk so consistently well anywhere else at all, with the possible exception of Las Vegas.

Toronto is the most racially mixed city in the world. Over half the city's population was born outside Canada and 100,000 new immigrants arrive each year. As a result, Toronto publishes information for its citizens in a remarkable 30 languages.

Naturally, this is reflected in the local cuisine, and the city's 7,000 restaurants are famously diverse. I mean, where else would you see a Hungarian/Thai restaurant (The Hungary Thai) or a Jamaican/Italian takeaway (Rasta Pasta)?

The most celebrated of all Toronto's restaurants is Canoe, a high temple of contemporary Canadian cuisine housed on the fifty-fourth floor of the TD Bank Tower in Wellington Street West. The grub here is utterly brilliant, each dish celebrating the culture of Canada's distinct provinces.

The wine list, too, is fabulous and stretches to 20 closely printed pages. All the classic wine regions of the world are represented, but much is made of Canada's increasingly fine wines – and quite right, too. There are around 30 Canadian whites on the list and ditto reds; plus 13 Canadian fizzes, of which the Benjamin Bridge vintage brut from Gaspereau Valley, Nova Scotia, is the most sought after despite being the priciest.

I'd never tried it before – I didn't even know they made wine in Nova Scotia. But at the sommelier's insistence I gave it a whirl and, goodness, I'm glad I did. It's astoundingly fine. Handcrafted from 100 per cent Chardonnay and made in the traditional method (which Canadians call *méthode classique*), it spends four years on the lees before disgorgement and release.

It's citrussy, nutty, toasty and even slightly savoury. It's also completely moreish and I struggle to believe that they've only been making fizz at Benjamin Bridge for barely 15 years.

Toronto is a long way to go for a drink. Happily, the wines of Benjamin Bridge are now available outside Canada. Do, for heaven's sake, seek them out.

WWW.BENJAMINBRIDGE.COM

ARMAND DE BRIGNAC
BLANC DE NOIRS NV

CHAMPAGNE, FRANCE

Right, brace yourselves: this is eye-wateringly expensive, most would say ridiculously so. I certainly made a right tit of myself when I first came across it and asked the price. On being told it was £695 (US$900), I assumed – not unreasonably, I reckon – that they meant £695 per dozen bottles rather than £695, erm, per one bottle. How thick could I be? My hackles rose further on seeing the flash metallic bottle. I was predisposed to hate the wine on every level. The thing is, dammit, that having tasted it, I loved it.

Armand de Brignac Champagne is produced by Jean-Jacques Cattier and his son, Alexandre. The family has been making wine in Champagne since 1763, and Jean-Jacques's own Cattier Champagne is extremely good. Head winemaker is Emilien Boutillat.

Although Cattier-made, the Armand de Brignac brand – more familiarly known as Ace of Spades thanks to the logo on said metallic gold, silver and pewter-coloured bottles – is owned by rapper Jay-Z, formerly the number-one fan of Roederer Cristal Champagne.

Jay-Z notoriously transferred his affections to Armand de Brignac, however, after having been slighted by Frédéric Rouzaud, MD of Louis Roederer Champagne. Rouzaud, on being asked what he thought about rappers and bling-meisters knocking back Cristal in nightclubs, replied in true Gerald Ratner, foot-in-the-mouth style: 'What can we do? We can't forbid people from buying it.'

Anyway, Jay-Z's association with Armand de Brignac and his later purchase of the brand has done it no harm whatsoever, and it's the fizz of choice of many a deep-pocketed A-list barfly. Crucially, though, it has also won plaudits from the critics and the Blanc de Noirs was recently acclaimed best in the world at a blind tasting of 250 *cuvées* held by *FINE Champagne Magazine* and tastingbook.com.

Made from 100 per cent Pinot Noir from *grands* and *premiers crus* vineyards only, it's marked by extraordinarily complex flavours, with rich, dark berry fruit, hints of spice, poached pears, mocha and baked brioche.

Only 2,333 bottles of it have been produced and, as I say, it's a bonkers price, I mean, just imagine what they charge in chic New York, LA or Cannes nightclubs! But if someone else is paying, drink deep and enjoy.

WWW.ARMANDDEBRIGNAC.COM

REMEMBER GENTLEMEN,
IT'S NOT JUST FRANCE
WE ARE FIGHTING FOR,
IT'S CHAMPAGNE!

WINSTON CHURCHILL

BROWN BROTHERS
ZIBIBBO ROSA NV

VICTORIA, AUSTRALIA

The last time I visited Brown Brothers in Milawa, north east of Melbourne, Australia, I was breathalyzed. At 9.30A.M.

I had enjoyed quite a bit of the legendary Brown Brothers hospitality the night before and I was lucky to pass the breath test. My travelling companion and navigator for the day, Mark Tower, had partied longer than I had and was clearly still way over the limit. Indeed, he took grave exception to the policeman being so unsporting as to whip out his breathalyzer on a Sunday morning and lost no time in telling him so. The cop gave me a wink and told me to drive straight on and find the babbling old fool a cold shower and a hot coffee.

It's Ned Kelly country round there, and the iron-clad bushranger met his end in a gunfight at Glenrowan in 1880, only a few kilometres from Milawa. Barely five years later, Scottish émigré John Francis Brown planted his first vines not far from Wangaratta ('Wang' to the locals), on the main Sydney to Melbourne road. The family firm was officially founded in 1889, and today it's run by JFB's grandchildren and great-grandchildren. They are famously innovative and at the last count Brown Bros had more than 100 wines on its list, made from a staggering 50 different grape varieties.

As far as fizz is concerned, they make several, including a lovely fresh vintage rosé; a Shiraz (fizzy reds are quite the thing in Oz); a Prosecco; and a Pinot Noir/Pinot Meunier/Chardonnay blend that's Australia's most-awarded non-vintage sparkler.

It's the Brown Bros Zibibbo Rosa that I keep coming back to, though. It's easy to sneer at its lack of sophistication and cheap price. I prefer to celebrate its frothy frivolity and the sheer joy of its uncomplicated, low-alcohol (7.5%vol) accessibility.

Zibibbo is the Italian name for the (white) Muscat of Alexandria grape, and this is blended with a splash of red Cienna – a cross between Sumoll and Cabernet Sauvignon – to give it its charming pink hue.

It's light, fruity and fun, with hints of wild strawberries and watermelon on nose and palate. Don't be snooty; you'll love it!

WWW.BROWNBROTHERS.COM.AU

CA'DEL BOSCO FRANCIACORTA CUVÉE ANNA MARIA CLEMENTI BRUT RISERVA 2007

FRANCIACORTA, ITALY

Franciacorta is the only sparkling wine in the world, apart from champagne, whose name refers not only to the wine itself, but also to the method and to the region of its production. Still wines – mainly red – have been made here for centuries, but it is only since the 1960s that sparklers have been produced, and only since the 1980s with any real purpose.

Denominazione di Origine Controllata or DOC status was granted in 1967, specifying that the wines should be made by said traditional method, using only hand-harvested Chardonnay (giving freshness and complexity), Pinot Nero (body and structure) and Pinot Bianco (creamy fresh fruit, softness and a light citrus acidity). *Denominazione di Origine Controllata e Garantita*, or DOCG, status followed in 1997. In 2003, however, Franciacorta became the only wine in Italy to be exempt from putting this *appellation* on its bottles. As with champagne – which also doesn't declare its *appellation* – the single word 'Franciacorta' is deemed enough to guarantee quality and place of origin.

And if you're in any doubt at all as to the quality of top Franciacorta, then just get your mitts on this. It's quite staggeringly fine and I can't imagine any fine-fizz-lover not being bowled over by it. Made from a blend of Chardonnay, Pinot Nero and Pinot Bianco, it spent almost nine years on the lees and is crisp, clean and fresh yet also savoury, toasty and spicy. It teases the palate with different layers of flavour being released with each mouthful.

Elegance, finesse and delicacy are Ca'del Bosco's watchwords, and this is as satisfying as they come – almost decadently so.

WWW.CADELBOSCO.COM

CA' DI RAJO MANZONI ROSA SPUMANTE EXTRA DRY 2015

VENETO, ITALY

Right, so this is quite a weird one. A deliciously dry pink fizz made from a grape variety nobody has ever heard of using a system of vine cultivation that doesn't exist any more. Confused? You will be.

Ca' di Rajo is a family-owned winery in Veneto, Italy. Founded in 1931, it's home to some really quite extreme and unusual winemaking. The company's 'Lemoss' semi-sparkling wine is a case in point. It's made from 100 per cent Glera (the grape that used to be known as Prosecco) using a method that hardly anybody else bothers with any more – the traditional so-called *col fondo* method. The wine is fermented in tank, just as all Prosecco is, but instead of staying in the tank, just before the fermentation finishes the wine is transferred to bottles, where the rest of the fermentation continues. It is left unfiltered and is therefore quite cloudy and is stored standing up in bottles sealed with crown caps. Locals pour it into jugs before serving, leaving the gunk at the bottom of the bottle. It's wonderfully authentic and marvellously tasty.

My favourite Ca' di Rajo wine, though, is this pink fizz made from 100 per cent Manzoni Rosa, a cross between Trebbiano and Gewurztraminer (there, I told you that nobody has heard of it). The grapevines are grown using the Bellussera system (nope, nor me) invented at the end of the nineteenth century in an effort to thwart downy mildew. It's hard to explain and you really need to see it for yourself, but basically the vines are grown a couple of metres off the ground on a system of linked iron cables. It really is quite a sight and I can't think of anyone or anywhere else that uses it.

Anyway, back to the fizz. It undergoes a long fermentation using the Charmat method and emerges in an impossibly pretty pink colour, light and delicate. There are hints of rose petals and Turkish Delight on the nose, while on the palate it's full of wild strawberry flavours, apricots and citrus but refreshingly bone-dry on the finish.

There really is no other wine like this. It's quirky, it's different and it's utterly, mouth-wateringly delicious.

WWW.CADIRAJO.IT

DOMAINE CARNEROS BRUT 2011

CALIFORNIA, USA

Domaine Carneros, surrounded by its immaculately tended vineyards and formal gardens, looks like nothing so much as a fine French château plucked from its rightful Gallic soil and plonked slap-dab in the middle of the Napa Valley. It seems both strangely out of place and remarkably at home and makes quite a sight for those driving along Highway 12-121 between Sonoma and Napa.

Domaine Chandon, set up by Moët & Chandon in 1973, was the first foray into California by a champagne house, and for many years the Taittinger family looked for the perfect site with which to emulate Moët. Finally Claude Taittinger purchased this estate in Carneros in 1982, in cahoots with Kobrand Corp. It's fair to say they've never looked back.

With winemaker Eileen Crane at the helm (she had worked previously at Domaine Chandon as assistant winemaker), Domaine Carneros produces exemplary Napa Valley fizz. All the estate vineyards are certified organic, and Domaine Carneros grows almost all – but not quite – the grapes it needs. A small amount needs to be bought from other quality minded growers.

There are eight sparkling wines in the Domaine Carneros range (and several still Chardonnays and Pinot Noirs), of which my favourite is this, the 2011 Domaine Carneros Brut. A blend of Chardonnay and Pinot Noir (half and half), made using the traditional method (of course), it's deliciously fruity with hints of pears, apples and peaches with a long creamy finish.

It's deeply refreshing and satisfying, and given the work that's gone into it and the noble Taittinger history behind it, it's jolly well priced, too.

WWW.DOMAINECARNEROS.COM

CHAMPAGNE BOTTLE SIZES

Champagne is well known for the impressive number of differently sized bottles in which it markets its fizz. These range from the minuscule quarter bottle, which holds a paltry, barely-enough-to-gargle-with 20cl, to the mighty, ask-all-the-neighbours-round Nebuchadnezzar, which holds a deeply satisfying 1,500cl – 20 full bottles – which is pretty much enough for us both to have a bath in.

Just for the record and for those swotting for their next pub quiz, here's the full list of champagne bottles that you might be lucky enough to come across:

QUARTER BOTTLE = 20CL

HALF BOTTLE = 37.5CL

BOTTLE = 75CL

MAGNUM = 2 BOTTLES

JEROBOAM = 4 BOTTLES

REHOBOAM = 6 BOTTLES

METHUSELAH = 8 BOTTLES

SALMANAZAR = 12 BOTTLES

BALTHAZAR = 16 BOTTLES

NEBUCHADNEZZAR = 20 BOTTLES

There is, however, a gap. There has been a faller by the wayside. Well, it didn't so much fall, as was pushed. The much-missed imperial pint which, containing an exact 56.8cl, sat snugly between the half bottle and bottle, was once the UK's most popular size of champagne bottle, favoured by all the finest restaurants, hotels, clubs and bars until it was outlawed by EU killjoys.

The Imp's most famous devotee was Sir Winston Churchill, who deemed it just enough for two people to drink at lunch and for one person to drink at dinner and who was said to carry a bottle of it around in his greatcoat pocket during visits to Blitz-hit London. The great man's favourite brand was, as we all know, Pol Roger, and he drank an imperial pint of it every day, in between his whisky and his brandy.

'Clemmie thinks that a full bottle is too much for me,' he once said of his wife. 'But I know that half a bottle is insufficient to tease my brains. An imperial pint is an ideal size for a man like me. It pleases everyone, even the producer.'

Curiously enough, one of the unexpected results of our unexpected Brexit might well be the Imp's return. James Simpson MW, MD of Pol Roger Portfolio recently told me that not only had he already been in contact with Pol's glass manufacturer to discuss the possibility of restarting production of the Imp, but that he had also had a meeting about it with my old boss, Simon Berry, chairman of Berry Bros & Rudd, and – like James – a long-time advocate of the Imperial Pint.

Until such time, I'm going to make do with the magnum, not only because it looks impressive but also because the wine matures just that little bit more slowly and more elegantly within it. Oh, and because as Churchill himself once remarked: 'A magnum is the perfect size for two gentlemen over lunch, especially if one isn't drinking.'

'A SINGLE GLASS OF CHAMPAGNE IMPARTS A FEELING OF EXHILARATION. THE NERVES ARE BRACED; THE IMAGINATION IS STIRRED; THE WITS BECOME MORE NIMBLE.'

WINSTON CHURCHILL

CASTELLO BONOMI FRANCIACORTA BRUT SATÉN NV

FRANCIACORTA, ITALY

Franciacorta, in Lombardy, Italy, is a tiny wine region but it has grown remarkably fast. In 1972, there were just 200 hectares under vine; today there are 3,500. This will be the limit, though, since there is simply no more room in which to plant, added to which property prices are sky-high here and as any fool knows, you're going to make a heck of a lot more money building and selling houses than planting vineyards and selling wine.

There are just 119 producers of Franciacorta, making some 18 million bottles a year. Nearly all the wineries are small, family-owned operations and nearly all are organic. Indeed, Franciacorta boasts the highest proportion of organic wine producers in the world, with the stated aim of being totally organic by 2020.

Castello Bonomi makes much of the fact that it boasts the only château or castello in Franciacorta, and it's a striking edifice for sure, rising proudly from the forested slopes of Monte Orfano. The region's calcerous soil is almost identical to that of Champagne, and the southern aspect of the vines is perfect for optimum ripeness. And the Castello Bonomi wines are spot-on, with this award-winning Satén being an absolute belter.

The term Satén is peculiar to Franciacorta. To qualify for the name, the wine must be a *blanc de blancs* (made from white grapes only – in this case Chardonnay – and/or Pinot Bianco) and it must be ever so slightly less fizzy than normal (4.5 atmospheres of pressure rather than 6).

With delicate notes of tropical fruits, acacia honey, wild flowers and baked bread, it's lusciously enticing and rewarding and – with its very fine and gentle sparkle – very palatable.

WWW.CASTELLOBONOMI.IT

JOSEPH CATTIN
CRÉMANT D'ALSACE BRUT NV

ALSACE, FRANCE

Alsace has it all. An astonishingly beautiful region of rolling hills, forests, ruined castles and exquisite medieval towns and villages such as Colmar, Obernai, Ribeauvillé and Riquewihr, it's a balmy spot, blessed with the lowest rainfall in all of France. It boasts an excellent and hearty cuisine (*choucroute garnie, tarte flambée* or buttered white asparagus, anyone?) and more Michelin-starred restaurants than anywhere in the country other than Paris.

And, of course, Alsace has it wines. These range from bone-dry whites to off-dry and sumptuously sweet ones to rival any fine Sauternes, Tokaji or Trockenbeerenauslese – from smooth, supple cherry-ripe reds to crisp and refreshing traditional method crémants or sparklers. Oh, and Alsace also has some of tastiest, most varied and downright seductive *eaux de vie* you'll come across anywhere else in the world.

Of all its wines, though, it's the Crémants d'Alsace that are the least well known – at least over here in the UK – and I can't for the life of me think why, because they are superbly drinkable and ridiculously well priced. Indeed, they are the most popular fizzes in France after those of Champagne.

My current favourite comes from Joseph Cattin, a family-owned house (like almost all Alsace wineries) founded in 1720, which is pretty recent for Alsace, where wineries founded in the mid-1600s still abound. A blend of hand-harvested, low-yielding Pinot Blanc and Auxerrois Blanc, the Joseph Cattin Crémant d'Alsace Brut NV might only be the house's entry-level fizz, but it's a right charmer, being light, fresh and fruity with a fine mousse. It has that delectable creaminess that you find in the white wines of Alsace, along with delicious notes of crisp green apple and citrus.

It makes the perfect apéritif but also goes well with simple fish dishes and even, as I discovered to my delight on my most recent visit, with the traditional Alsace apple tart.

WWW.CATTIN.FR

CAVICCHIOLI LAMBRUSCO ROSATO DOLCE NV

EMILIA-ROMAGNA, ITALY

Ah, Lambrusco! Takes you back, doesn't it? Back to the days of Black Tower and Blue Nun Liebfraumilch, and of Piat d'Or, Mateus Rosé and Hirondelle; back to Watney's Red Barrel, Babycham, Harvey Wallbangers, Tequila Sunrises and Piña Coladas. If you were born after 1970, you won't have a clue what I'm going on about. If you were, you will know only too well.

When I had my first holiday job in Oddbins wine shop in 1977, we sold Lambrusco by the crate-load but could hardly shift any of the Wallaby White and Kanga Rouge, the only Australian wines we stocked in those days. I think it's fair to say that the alcoholic landscape has changed somewhat.

Lambrusco is not only the name of the wine but also of the grape from which it is made. It comes from Emilia-Romagna (mainly) and Lombardy (a bit) in northern Italy and, thankfully, has nothing to do with Lambrini, an extraordinarily unpleasant sparkling perry (pear cider) made, so I believe, in Liverpool.

As I say, Lambrusco was all the rage in the 1970s and then became frightfully passé. It's now creeping back into fashion and not just because anything from the Seventies is now seen as retro and cool, but because the best Lambrusco is really rather good.

I don't think there are any better examples than this one from Cavicchioli, one of the leading producers, founded in 1928. It's made by the tank or Charmat method and is deep pink, frothy rather than fizzy, and full of ripe strawberry and raspberry flavours. It's low in alcohol (just 7.5%vol) and high in sugar (with 55 grams per litre) and just lovely when served well chilled with vanilla ice cream. It is also scrumptious drunk alongside great salty chunks of fine Parmigiano-Reggiano.

Go on, dust off your cheesecloth shirt and flared denims and give it a whirl.

WWW.CAVICCHIOLI.IT

CHANDON ROSÉ NV

MENDOZA, ARGENTINA

Moët & Chandon's tentacles stretch everywhere. Not only is Moët the best-selling champagne of all, the company also has sparkling wine outposts as far afield as Brazil (established in 1973), California (1973), Australia (1986), India (2013) and China (2014).

Moët's first foreign foray, though, was in Argentina, where it set up Bodegas Chandon in 1959. It was a far-sighted move. Argentina might be the world's fifth-largest wine producer today, famed in particular for its wonderful, violet-scented Malbecs, but in the 1950s I think it's fair to say it was something of a vinous backwater.

Bodegas Chandon lies in the heart of Mendoza, where chalky soils, hot days and cool nights not only result in world-class red wines but in fine sparklers, too. This pale-pink example, which only launched in the UK in 2014, is my favourite: a blend of Chardonnay and Pinot Noir with an added splash of Malbec. This latter grape – originally from Cahors, in France, where it's responsible for the region's celebrated 'Black Wine' – might be Argentina's most successful and important red grape (although Bonarda is the most widely grown), but I can't ever remember having come across it being used in a sparkler before. In France, the grape stays on the vine for around 100 days, while in Argentina it's about 150 days – meaning that it's riper, softer and less tannic, and it certainly adds a little something to this blend: colour of course, but also a delicate, elusive, floral perfume.

The fizz, made in the traditional method, has juicy, summery, citrus and wild- and sour-cherry fruit on the palate, with a notable and thrilling freshness. It's not badly priced for a champagne substitute and is well worth seeking out.

WWW.CHANDON.COM.AR

CHAPEL DOWN KIT'S COTY CŒUR DE CUVÉE 2013

KENT, ENGLAND

I've always had a soft spot for Chapel Down, near Tenterden, Kent. I was brought up just down the road in Rolvenden and, although I live happily in Sussex these days, Kent is where my heart still lies. Of course, when I was growing up, we were surrounded by hop gardens and orchards. Today vineyards have largely taken their place, and it thrills me that God's Chosen County is making fizz of such class as Chapel Down.

Stubbornness and single-mindedness run deep hereabouts. Kent was the only county to stand up to the invading William, Duke of Normandy, and since he never conquered Kent, he was always referred to in our history lessons as King William, never William the Conqueror. It's a great story – Stigande, the archbishop of Canterbury, and Egelsine, abbot of St. Augustine's, barred William's way to the capital after his victory at Hastings with a handful of Kentish nobles and serfs, offering him peace or war. He chose the former and let Kent be: unconquered and free to enjoy its ancient liberties. *Invicta*, meaning unvanquished, is the county motto.

Anyway, I digress horribly. Chapel Down is the UK's largest wine producer and, with a massive expansion underway, soon to overtake Denbies, in Surrey, in terms of vineyard acreage, too. MD Mark Harvey was formerly a director of Moët-Hennessy. This tells you something about the state of English wine, given that he'd rather look after Chapel Down than Moët or Veuve Clicquot. In Josh Donaghay-Spire he has a supremely gifted winemaker.

And, gosh, Chapel Down's wines are good. Of their fizzes, I've drunk far more than my fair share of the Classic NV Brut. But with the brand-new 2013 Kit's Coty Cœur de Cuvée, England's first £100/US$130-a-bottle wine (only 130 cases produced), Chapel Down has really hit the bullseye. Made from the heart of the first pressing of exceptional-quality Chardonnay, it's stunning, full of cream, toast, nuts, fresh ripe apples and baked ones, too, backed by the longest of finishes.

If this doesn't persuade you that England makes world-class fizz, nothing will.

WWW.CHAPELDOWN.COM

CHAPOUTIER LA MUSE DE RW BRUT NATURE 2012

RHÔNE VALLEY, FRANCE

I think it's generally accepted by those who know him that the maverick maestro of the Rhône, Michel Chapoutier, is nothing if not passionate. He cares deeply about – and has strong opinions upon – just about everything, and to spend time with him can be an exhausting but hugely uplifting experience. I guarantee that within 60 minutes Michel will have touched upon wine (natch), food, art, music, poetry and goodness knows what else, and all in quite some detail.

When I first met him I felt as if I'd been buffeted by an intellectual French whirlwind. We sat on the terrace of his fifteenth-century house overlooking the Rhône Valley as he discoursed upon this and that, pouring half-finished glasses of fine wine over the terrace, so keen was he to move on to the next one. And in between bottles, he conducted vigorously a recording of Saint-Saëns's *Organ Symphony*, which blasted out over the valley at full bore.

According to Michel, if you like wine and if you like music, you will like them both twice as much if you enjoy them together. Which means, I suppose, that you should crack open this bottle only once you've teed up *Parsifal*, *Lohengrin* or *Tannhäuser* on the stereo – the 'RW' in the wine's name referring to none other than Richard Wagner, a devoted customer of Marius Chapoutier, Michel's great-grandfather.

I'm sure Herr Wagner would have loved this. Indeed, I can't imagine anyone not devouring it. A 100-per-cent Marsanne made in the traditional method and aged for three years on the lees, it comes from St-Péray, a tiny *appellation* of the northern Rhône, whose sparkling wines were once prized more highly than those of Champagne.

It's fresh, fruity and herb-tinged. There are notes of honeysuckle, nuts and apricots and it has a long, savoury finish. It's such lovely stuff that I'm certain you'll enjoy it without the need to have Wagner booming in the background. On the other hand, maybe just a quick blast of the *Meistersingers* overture might be just the ticket.

WWW.CHAPOUTIER.COM

HENRI CHAUVET
BLANC DE NOIRS BRUT NV

CHAMPAGNE, FRANCE

Henri Chauvet, run by Damien and Mathilde Chauvet, is a tiny artisanal producer of absolutely first-rate champagne in the quiet and very pretty *premier cru* village of Rilly-la-Montagne near Reims. It's not to be confused with Marc Chauvet, who is Henri's little brother and whose winery is almost opposite, run by Marc's children (Clotilde making the wine and Nicolas tending the vines), excellent though the wines are.

I first came across Henri Chauvet at a *Spectator* tasting hosted by our old mates Amanda Skinner and Laura Taylor of Private Cellar, one of our partners in the *Spectator* Wine Club and stockists of Chauvet's fizzes ever since Private Cellar set up shop in 2004. We had around 30 readers at the tasting, there to sample a couple of dozen wines and whittle them down to a sensible six, which we could then offer in our magazine to the wider readership. Readers' Wines rather than Readers' Wives.

The absolute runaway winner was this, Henri Chauvet's Blanc de Noirs Brut NV. The readers positively lapped it up. The tasting being held the day after press day, one or two folk from *Spectator* editorial drifted by with more time on their hands than was good for them and, carrying a bit of a thirst, they lapped it up as well. It was thumbs-up all round.

My favourite comment was from a reader who declared it the best champagne he'd ever had and that it was 'far too good to waste on the in-laws'. And it is indeed a cracking wine and proves just how good a grower's champagne can be and just how well-priced they are when compared to the big houses, the so-called *grandes marques*.

The Chauvets make their wine in a very traditional manner and still riddle their bottles by hand in their chalk cellars. They only disgorge the wines when they need to prepare a shipment. Made from 90 per cent Pinot Noir and 10 per cent Pinot Meunier, the current blend is based on the 2013 and 2014 vintages and is crisp, clean and fresh. There's also a nice touch of toasty biscuit in there, too, and a very fine mousse.

It's grower's champagne at its best.

WWW.CHAMPAGNE-CHAUVET.COM

COATES & SEELY BRUT RESERVE NV

HAMPSHIRE, ENGLAND

As managing director of AXA Millésimes (the vineyard-owning arm of AXA Insurance), based in Bordeaux and tasked with finding underperforming wine estates in which to invest, develop and turn around, Christian Seely has an enviable record. Not only did he famously revive the fortunes of Quinta do Noval in Portugal's Douro Valley, he also restored to glory such blue-chip estates as Château Pichon-Baron and Château Pibran in Pauillac, Château Suduiraut in Sauternes, Château Petit-Village in Pomerol, Domaine de l'Arlot in Burgundy, Château Belles Eaux in the Languedoc, and Tokaji producer Disznókó in Hungary. In short, Seely is no slouch.

But it's all very well travelling the world, buying estates with someone else's money. Where in the world would Christian Seely choose to make his own wine? Bordeaux? Burgundy? Champagne? Napa? Er, nope: Hampshire.

As I say, Seely knows his onions and long ago realized that there are places in southern England that are ideal for the production of first-rate sparkling wine. And that's what he wanted to do: make the finest-possible English fizz. He joined forces with an old business-school chum, Nicholas Coates, and after much searching found the ideal spot: an existing eight-hectare vineyard in a chalky valley in north Hampshire, made famous by the novel *Watership Down*. Coates & Seely formed a partnership with the vineyard's owner, Daphne Cunningham, and planted a further seven hectares.

The result, ten years later, is this magnificent fizz: Coates & Seely Brut Reserve NV. They also make a rosé and a *blanc de blancs* (total production is just 5,000 cases a year), but it's this 65 per cent Chardonnay and 35 per cent Pinot Noir blend that I admire the most. No, not admire the most – love the most, for it's a beauty. A blend of the 2009 and 2010 vintages, aged for three years before release, it's dry but richly flavoured, with wild berry fruits and crunchy English apple tones. There's honey in the background, and whispers of toasty brioche.

Given that Coates & Seely took four trophies, including Supreme Champion, at the inaugural 2017 UK Wine Awards, it's clear that Christian hasn't lost his magic touch.

WWW.COATESANDSEELY.COM

CODORNÍU CUVÉE BARCELONA BRUT NV

PENEDÈS, SPAIN

We British can't seem to get enough of Cava, the celebrated (or notorious, depending on your view) sparkling wine of Penedès in Spain. Cava (the Catalan word for 'cellar') comprises a whopping 40 per cent (and growing) of all sparkling wine retail sales in the UK, which is an awful lot of Spanish fizz.

The top-selling brand in Spain, and in UK supermarkets, both in terms of volume and value, is Codorníu, a family-owned company founded in 1551 (it's the seventeenth-oldest such company in the world) and still going strong. Codorníu is the proud owner of Europe's largest family-owned single vineyard, all 2,245 hectares of it, and has some claim to be Cava's originator, producing its first commercial example in 1872. And with the company currently enjoying annual worldwide sales of a staggering 60 million bottles, it must be doing something right.

I must confess that Cava has never been my favourite fizz, but with the recent growth in the number of tapas bars outside Spain and the surge in interest in Spanish cuisine, I find I've been knocking the stuff back much more of late.

Cava is made by the same method as champagne and was even called 'champagne' until Champagne protected itself and Spain joined the EU. Ninety per cent of the stuff is made in the Penedès, although the Cava DO, set up in 1986, is unique in Spain, in that it covers several geographical areas rather than just one – permitting small outposts of production in places such as Valencia, Extremadura, Rioja and Navarra – as well as regulating the varieties that might be used, the length of ageing and method of production.

The Codorníu Cuvée Barcelona NV is as good a place as any to start working out whether you like Cava. Made from a blend of Parellada, Macabeu and Xarel-lo it's crisp, light, refreshing and fruity with plenty of crunchy apple flavours and touches of citrus.

It's a pretty bottle, too, strangely reminiscent of Perrier-Jouët's Belle Epoque (see page 117), although my wife, who knows about such things, reckons it's a ranunculus sprawling all over the bottle rather than PJ's famous Japanese anemone. The bottles probably look conveniently the same in the dark of a Barcelona nightclub, though.

WWW.CODORNIU.COM

'MY ONLY REGRET IS THAT I HAVE NOT DRUNK MORE CHAMPAGNE IN MY LIFE.'

JOHN MAYNARD KEYNES

DOMAINE COLLIN
CRÉMANT DE LIMOUX
BRUT CUVÉE ROSÉ NV

LANGUEDOC, FRANCE

My maths has always been terrible, but by my back-of-the-envelope calculation, they were making sparkling wines in Limoux, deep in the heart of the Languedoc, almost 140 years before they had worked out how to do it in Champagne. The first recorded mention of fizz in these parts dates back to 1531. Dom Pérignon – even if not exactly the inventor of sparkling champagne, at least its most famous pioneer – didn't even become cellarer at the Abbaye Saint-Pierre d'Hautvillers until 1668.

The *appellation* for Crémant de Limoux was created in 1990. Chardonnay and Chenin Blanc are its main grape varieties, with Pinot Noir and the traditional local variety – Mauzac – permitted in small quantities. Conversely, the AC for the region's other sparkler – Blanquette de Limoux – insists that Mauzac comprises at least 90 per cent of the blend and Pinot Noir is *verboten*.

This deliciously fine, pink Crémant de Limoux is a bottle-fermented blend of all the above save the Mauzac. It's full of lush, ripe raspberries and wild strawberries but, with only 6 grams of residual sugar per litre (gpl), brut champagne usually starts at around 9gpl; it's gratifyingly dry on the finish.

Producer Philippe Collin knows a thing or two about sparkling wine production, having been born in Champagne as the second son of a winemaker. He decamped to the Languedoc in search of decent weather and some land that was a fraction of what it costs in Champagne. He planted his vines around the village of Tourreilles, a 40-minute drive southwest of Carcassonne, and has never looked back. This is a charming wine and I love the stripy retro label, too. Best of all, I love the price, which is ridiculously low.

WWW.VIE-D-OC.FR/VIN-DOMAINE-COLLIN

'THERE COMES A TIME IN EVERY WOMAN'S LIFE WHEN THE ONLY THING THAT HELPS IS A GLASS OF CHAMPAGNE.'

BETTE DAVIS IN *OLD ACQUAINTANCE*

THE CO-OPERATIVE
LES PIONNIERS CHAMPAGNE NV

CHAMPAGNE, FRANCE

Supermarket champagne is big business. Not only do all the supermarkets sell ailing or poorly performing *grandes marques* champagnes by the van-load using their notorious discount deals, but they also all have their own-label champagnes in several different styles – brut NV, *blanc de blancs*, vintage and so on.

To be honest, I'm not usually a huge fan of supermarket champagnes. All too often they're made by second-rate producers from the second or third pressing of the least-good-quality grapes from the least-good sites in the least-good vineyards. The wines are then aged for the bare legal minimum before release and they rarely do anything to add lustre to the good name of champagne. As a rule, I'd rather spend a bit more and have a decent so-called grower's champagne, or go without for a bit and survive on Prosecco or crémant until I can afford one of the big names.

Occasionally, though, I remind myself to stop being such a cynic and such a snob and buy a bottle of the Co-op's Les Pionniers. They won't tell you, but I can, that it's made by none other than Piper-Heidsieck and the wizard that is Régis Camus, winner of the Sparkling Winemaker of the Year accolade at the International Wine Challenge a record eight times.

This fizz is an award-winner too, picking up gongs both at the *Decanter* World Wine Awards and the International Wine Challenge. And, for a sub-twenty-quid champagne it's really very good indeed. If you can be bothered to buy a few bottles and leave them alone for six to twelve months, it'll be even better.

Either way, it's great value and is my pick of the pops when it comes to supermarket own-label champagne.

WWW.CO-OPERATIVEFOOD.CO.UK

DELAMOTTE BRUT NV

CHAMPAGNE, FRANCE

A couple of years ago I enjoyed a riotous week swanning around the Mediterranean with a group of bibulous *Spectator* readers. There were four of us from the magazine plus 40 readers and we had a complete and utter hoot.

We sailed from Venice to Athens on board Cunard's *Queen Victoria*, and I don't think I — or anyone else – drew a sober breath during the entire voyage. The figures will back me up when I say I pulled my weight: at the end of the week, I got a drinks bill for US$843.

Needless to say, we drank a heck of a lot of champagne and it was chocks away from the very first glass. Beautifully chilled, the fizz was soft, creamy and gently honeyed. I remember stopping in mid-conversation to ask the waiter what brand it was, as it was so delicious. It turned out to be Delamotte, Cunard's pouring brand, supplied to the company by Corney & Barrow, no less.

It's a fabulous wine and had us all billing and cooing over it during that first drinks party. Delamotte was founded in 1760, making it the fifth-oldest champagne house. It is famously the sister house to mighty Salon, one of the finest and rarest champagnes that money can buy. I've only ever drunk Salon once in my life, but I've never forgotten it. Salon is a vintage-only champagne, made from just one grape (Chardonnay), from just one village (Le Mesnil-sur-Oger) in just one year. And if a vintage isn't declared, they don't make any. In which case – and here's the thing – the grapes go to Delamotte.

As a result, crafty connoisseurs keep an eye out for Delamotte vintage champagne in years that Salon decides not to make any. I think that overcomplicates things, and ever since our *Spectator* cruise, I have simply been making a beeline for the Delamotte Brut NV.

I certainly drank bucketloads on board the *Queen Vic*. It was on offer for US$55 a bottle, which compared very favourably with the US$475 Cunard wanted for a bottle of 2002 Salon. And which would you rather have – one bottle of 2002 Salon or almost nine of Delamotte?

WWW.SALONDELAMOTTE.COM

'TOO MUCH OF ANYTHING IS BAD, BUT TOO MUCH CHAMPAGNE IS JUST RIGHT.'

F. SCOTT FITZGERALD

DENBIES GREENFIELDS 2011

SURREY, ENGLAND

Denbies Wine Estate near Dorking, Surrey, which celebrated its thirtieth anniversary in 2016, is as much a tourist attraction as it is a winery.

And it really is quite a striking attraction at that. There you are tootling through leafy Surrey along the Reigate Road; you turn north onto the A24 and head towards Leatherhead and then left onto Bradley Lane and all of a sudden there you are in the Napa Valley (or Margaret River or Hawke's Bay or some such). You're surrounded by vines (all 107 hectares of them) as far as the eye can see in every direction and there, at the heart of it all, is a vast New World-like winery-cum-visitor centre.

Well, I say visitor centre; it's rather more than that, for it also includes a winery shop, a farm shop, a brewery shop (oh, and a brewery: the Surrey Hills), along with the self-service Conservatory Restaurant and the rather posher Gallery Restaurant on the third floor with its 360-degree views. There are indoor tours and outdoor tours; there are 11km (7 miles) of footpaths through the vines where you can wander, cycle or even take the vineyard train; and if it's raining there's a cinema in which to watch a film on Denbies and English winemaking.

It's fair to say, then, that as far as wine tourism is concerned, Denbies has got it nailed. Whether they've nailed their winemaking quite so successfully is slightly more debatable, for their wines get a bit of a mixed press, with many critics labelling them dull and unexciting.

Well, I don't care what they say. I'll admit that I'm not a huge fan of the Denbies still wines, but I like their fizzes and I really like this one. A traditional method blend of the classic champagne grapes, it's full of fresh- and baked-apple aromas and flavours and a beautifully judged hint of toast and zesty citrus. It was a worthy winner of the gold medal at the 2016 International Wine Challenge.

Denbies deserves a huge pat on the back for helping put English winemaking and English wine tourism on the map. It also deserves a hearty pat for this delicious fizz, too.

WWW.DENBIES.CO.UK

DEVAUX ULTRA D NV

CHAMPAGNE, FRANCE

I've always really enjoyed the wines of Veuve A. Devaux, a fine champagne cooperative (founded in 1846 and formerly family-owned) that's usually known simply as Devaux. Its sleek, slender bottles are very distinctive, and the wines they contain are just as stylish and elegant.

I remember once being unaccountably upgraded to business class on an Air France flight to Caracas, of all places, and being plied regularly with the Devaux Grande Réserve Brut. I was so astonished by my good fortune that I drank way more than was good for me and, as the flight wore on, I couldn't help but think that this was definitely the best of all possible worlds and that on the whole, everything was really rather fabulous. It's unlikely to happen again, sadly, and has spoiled me forever. I've had a fondness for the brand, though, ever since.

It's a tricky business choosing the right wines to be served at 35,000 feet. Thanks to low humidity and cabin pressure, the astringent tannins and acidity in wine become more pronounced, apparently, and the effect of dehydration alters our perception of smell. As a result, you need wines that are fruit-driven and well-balanced, with soft tannins and good acidity. The champagnes of Devaux more than measure up, as you will see with this exceptional ultra brut. It's not a style of champagne that I'm hugely enamoured with as a rule, finding that fizzes with no dosage at all can be terribly sharp and austere.

With the Devaux Ultra D, however, everything is in harmony. The house is known for the fine quality and vibrancy of its fruit, and this blend of 60 per cent Pinot Noir and 40 per cent Chardonnay is perfectly brought into focus by a dosage of just 3 grams of sugar per litre. This very low (but, crucially, not zero) dosage and five years' ageing allow the juicy pear- and apple-like fruit and faint toastiness to shine, leading to a supremely fine glass of fizz.

And best of all, given that you can find Devaux's fizzes in mainstream bottle shops, you don't have to fly all the way to Caracas via Paris to enjoy it.

WWW.CHAMPAGNE-DEVAUX.FR

BIOWEINGUT DIWALD
GRÜNER VELTLINER SEKT 2012

LOWER AUSTRIA

I used to travel to Austria a lot to visit my eccentric but adored godmother, who lived in Petronell-Carnuntum, about as far to the east of the country as you can go before reaching Slovakia. She lived in a former forester's cottage in the shadow of a crumbling seventeenth-century *schloss* accompanied by an ever-changing succession of cats – most of which had been lured away from her neighbours by strategically placed saucers of milk and the promise of little slivers of ham and a warm sofa.

English-born, my godmother read *The Times* every morning and had tea every afternoon on the lawn or by the fireside, depending on the season. Austrian by adoption, she drank formidable amounts of wine produced and delivered by the local *winzer*, Josef Pimpel.

I was more than happy to help her in this task and we hoovered as much Grüner Veltliner, Silvaner, Blaufränkisch and Zweigelt as Herr Pimpel could deliver (which he did weekly, in litre bottles). He would peer round the door on his visits to see who else was in the house, unable to believe that my godmother and I could polish off so many bottles on our own.

Our favourite wine by far was his Grüner Veltliner and I've never lost my taste for this wonderful grape. Austria's signature variety, it somehow manages to combine the lusciousness of Pinot Gris, the bouquet of Riesling and the acidity of Sauvignon Blanc.

I know my godmother would have loved this sparkling example as much as I do. A so-called *Sekt* (the name given by Austrians and Germans to their sparkling wines, whatever their manner of production), this is certified organic and is made in the traditional method by Martin Diwald in Grossriedenthal in Lower Austria, 50km (31 miles) northwest of Vienna. And although not labelled as such, it's from a single vintage: 2012.

It's full-flavoured and fruity, and although it makes a perfect apéritif, it also partners all manner of dishes in a way that is typical of Grüner Veltliner, famous as being one of the most food-friendly of grapes.

WWW.WEINGUT-DIWALD.AT

DOM PÉRIGNON P2 1998

CHAMPAGNE, FRANCE

Dom Pérignon, usually known by its aficionados simply as 'DP', is not only the most celebrated of all *prestige cuvée* champagnes, it is also the first, having launched in 1926 with the 1921 vintage. Everyone's heard of it and everyone aspires to drink it.

But not everyone realizes that it's the *prestige cuvée* of Moët & Chandon. It's seen as a brand in itself – a stand-alone wine – unlike, say, Pol Roger, whose range leads directly to its Cuvée Sir Winston Churchill; Veuve Clicquot and its La Grande Dame; and, most famously, Louis Roederer and its Cristal. Moët does very little to suggest that it has anything to do with DP. Indeed, the company has separate winemakers: Benoît Gouez goes about his business as winemaker at Moët and Richard Geoffroy, 'Dr Feelgood' himself – he trained as a GP and the very day he qualified, he resigned to become a winemaker – is chef de cave at Dom Pérignon.

Notoriously, Moët also keeps shtum about how much Dom Pérignon is actually made. Wine-trade estimates put it at around five million bottles (compared to 500,000 or so bottles of Roederer Cristal or 1.5 million bottles total production at Pol Roger), which hardly makes it rare and exclusive. But I reckon this couldn't matter less, for Dom Pérignon is very, very good indeed. If anything, it proves how exceptional a winemaker Richard Geoffroy is, given that he can make something so utterly wonderful in such vast quantities.

OK, so this is the complicated bit. DP is made in exceptional years only and released after several years' maturation. A number of bottles from each vintage are also held back to age even longer on the lees. These are then released at a later date as that vintage's *plénitude deuxième*, or 'second age' (aka P2). The 1998 DP P2 (the current release) is exactly the same wine as the 1998 DP, which was originally released in 2005, except that it has had 16 years on the lees rather than seven, giving it greater depth and character.

As Dr Feelgood himself says, 'It sings higher and stronger'. And it is indeed an extraordinary wine: rich, biscuity, nutty and toasty with a seemingly endless finish. Wow!

WWW.DOMPERIGNON.COM

FERGHETTINA FRANCIACORTA BRUT ROSÉ 2012

FRANCIACORTA, ITALY

I can't imagine anyone not being completely seduced by this effervescent beauty: by its uniquely shaped, square-bottomed and really rather flash bottle; by its beguiling pale, salmon-pink colour; by its gentle, frothy fizz; and by its almost thirst-quenching palatability.

I first tasted it in the swanky surrounds of Michelin-starred Due Colombe, in Borgonato, Corte Franca, in the heart of Franciacorta. I glugged down a glass while perusing the menu and immediately ordered another, so scrumptious was it. But, wary of falling into the trap we've all plunged into before of soaking up some local vino abroad, buying some to take back home, tasting it and wondering what the heck we were thinking, I tried it again on a rainy winter's day in Brighton. If anything, I liked it even more. I ended up buying a case, my only regret being not buying more.

Ferghettina, the estate of which is strikingly situated high above Lake Iseo, Lombardy, produces exemplary Franciacorta and is not only one of the region's finest producers but also one of the largest. The company was founded in 1991 by Roberto Gatti, who had previously spent 20 years as the cellarmaster and viticulturalist at Bellavista (see page 30). He has since been joined by his children, Laura and Matteo.

To make this wonderful pink fizz, hand-picked, gently pressed Pinot Nero is fermented and left in stainless-steel vats over winter, waiting to be blended in the spring. The blending and second fermentation follow, after which the wine is left on the lees for three years. The result is a fizz of dazzling complexity and style, full of rose hips, wild strawberries, liquorice, pepper, spice and even something a little savoury and saline, almost like marsh samphire.

WWW.FERGHETTINA.IT

NICOLAS FEUILLATTE BRUT NV

CHAMPAGNE, FRANCE

Moët & Chandon might be the best-selling champagne brand in the world, but the fizz that the French themselves like the most is Nicolas Feuillatte. It has long been the country's best-selling champagne brand and is currently the third best-selling champagne brand in the world.

Of course, the name of the brand and the clever marketing behind it might lead one to think that it's a small, boutique brand, and it was indeed founded by a Monsieur Nicolas Feuillatte in 1971. He sold out in 1986, though, and the Centre Vinicole-Champagne Nicolas Feuillatte (CV-CNF) is now a truly massive enterprise, the largest cooperative union in Champagne, comprising 82 co-ops made up of 5,000 wine-growers with access to 2,250 hectares of vines. It's vast.

The CV-CNF operates from a veritable Cape Canaveral/James Bond villain's lair of a winery, just outside Épernay, that's so modern and efficient that it bottles fizz on behalf of several *grandes marques* houses. But do you know what? The wines aren't at all bad. Indeed, I would go further and say the Brut NV, aged for two years before release, is extremely reliable and a staple of many supermarkets and perfectly acceptable for drinks parties, family gatherings and piss-ups.

The Brut Rosé, too, is great value, especially when you take advantage of the inevitable price deals that surround it. If you want to push the boat out, though, try the 2006 Nicolas Feuillatte Palmes d'Or, its top-of-the-range *prestige cuvée* blended from 60 per cent Chardonnay and 40 per cent Pinot Noir and aged for nine years before release. It's a peach, all right, and has won several medals at very decent wine competitions.

WWW.NICOLAS-FEUILLATTE.COM

FREIXENET CASA SALA BRUT NATURE GRAN RESERVA 2007

PENEDÈS, SPAIN

Freixenet, founded in 1889 by the Ferrer and Sala families, is the bitter rival of Codorníu (see page 58), and the two companies dominate the Cava market. It's most famous for its jet-black bottles of Cordon Negro Cava, first launched in 1974, and for making a colossal 120 million bottles of Cava a year. Indeed, Freixenet – still family owned – makes more traditional method fizz than anyone else in the world, and also boasts sparkling wine vineyards in Argentina, Australia, California and Mexico, not to mention still-wine vineyards elsewhere in Spain.

This *gran reserva* is Freixenet's *prestige cuvée*, produced at the Ferrer family's old Casa Sala villa where the company's story began. Made from a blend of the traditional Cava grape varieties Parellada and Xarel-lo, the proportions of which depend on vintage conditions, it's hand-harvested and then pressed in a centuries-old wine press that first saw service in Champagne. Only around 1,500 cases are year are produced.

My wife always claims Cava smells of wet cardboard, teenage boys' socks and – I'm afraid she's not one to mince her words – farts. This, though, gets a resolute thumbs-up from Mrs Ray, although she did quail a bit at the price, reasoning that she could spend the same and get a more-than-decent champagne.

I would say that if you're a fan of Cava, this definitely warrants a taste; it's beautifully made, the quality is first rate and it's rare. But would you take it to someone's house as a gift? Unless they really know their wines they might assume – given that everyday Cava can be picked up for little more than a fiver – that you'd picked it up for a song in the supermarket.

It always astonishes me that entry-level Cava is so damn cheap, especially given that it's made by the expensive and time-consuming traditional method. But with total annual worldwide sales of 245 million bottles, Cava producers can charge peanuts and still make a fortune. I suggest slapping a ribbon on this example and bunging it in a box if you're giving it to someone. Just to be sure they understand that it didn't cost you peanuts.

WWW.FREIXENET.ES

GOSSET GRANDE RÉSERVE BRUT NV

CHAMPAGNE, FRANCE

Gosset, founded in 1584 and now owned by the Cointreau family, is famous not only for being the longest-established wine producer in all Champagne (it's not the longest-established sparkling wine producer in Champagne, don't forget; that's Ruinart, founded a full 145 years later) but also for making some really fine fizz.

The house was founded in the small Champagne village of Ay, where it still maintains a presence, rubbing shoulders with the likes of Ayala, Bollinger and Deutz. In 2009, however, Gosset moved most of its operations to new offices and cellars in Épernay.

When I worked at Berry Bros & Rudd all those years ago, we got through buckets of Gosset – we all loved it so much. We weren't so keen on the bottles themselves, though, because their distinctive, sloping-shouldered shape – based on the champagne bottles of yore – made them buggers to stack, and thanks to their thin necks, the foil capsules were always slipping off or getting torn. They still are.

But I quibble, for the fizz inside the bottles is fabulous, especially inside that of Gosset's standard-bearer: the Grande Réserve Brut. A blend of three vintages (2005, 2006 and 2007, I'm pretty sure) and of three grapes (45 per cent Chardonnay, 45 per cent Pinot Noir and 10 per cent Pinot Meunier), it's rich, creamy and toasty with ripe, red fruit and candied citrus. There's a mineral touch to it, too, and the promise of plenty of development to come.

I tucked away a couple of bottles in the cupboard under the stairs ages ago and drank them both recently and they were magnificent. The fizz had really filled out, softened and mellowed, bringing with it warm, toasty notes. I wish I could remember when I bought them, as I'd love to know how long they'd been there. Not that it matters. The point is that the Gosset's Grande Réserve Brut ages beautifully and doesn't need to knocked back in haste.

WWW.CHAMPAGNE-GOSSET.COM

LE GRAND SEUIL NV

PROVENCE, FRANCE

Just to be clear, this sparkler in its sleek, elegant bottle comes from the Château du Seuil in Provence, not the Château du Seuil in Bordeaux. Funnily enough, though, I do happen to know the wines of the latter estate and like them very much indeed. They're made by doctor-turned-winemaker Nicola Allison, who left Wales for general practice in New Zealand, only to give it up to make wine on her parents' estate on the banks of the River Garonne near Bordeaux. Sadly, for this book, Nicola only makes still reds and whites. If she made fizz I have no doubt at all that it would have been worthy of inclusion here.

Anyway, back to Provence or more specifically, back to 10km (6 miles) north of Aix-en-Provence and the other Château du Seuil, built in the early fourteenth century. It's a leader in wine tourism, and you can hike special trails through the vines here, visit its beautiful seventeenth-century formal gardens, and have simple meals and taste the wines on the terrace above the brand-new wine cellar. It's a gorgeous spot.

The 300-hectare estate produces a couple of very fine Cabernet Sauvignon, Grenache, Syrah still reds; a couple of still whites from Sauvignon Blanc, Grenache Blanc and Rolle; and a couple of still rosés from Grenache Noir, Cabernet Sauvigon and Cinsault. Its most recent addition to the range (released in early 2017) is this traditional method sparkler made from 100 per cent Ugni Blanc.

It's a corkingly fine wine. Although not madly complex, it has a delightfully aromatic nose, full of spring blossom and *garrigue*-like herbs and even a hint of elderflower. It's fresh and fruity on the palate, with juicy ripe pears and peaches followed by a long, bone-dry finish.

Provence doesn't really 'do' sparkling wines – rosé is the region's true forte – but this is a joy and it's just such a shame there aren't more like it.

WWW.CHATEAUDUSEUIL.FR

'HERE'S TO CHAMPAGNE, THE DRINK DIVINE, THAT MAKES US FORGET OUR TROUBLES.'

EDITHE LEA CHASE AND W.E.P. FRENCH,
WAES HAEL: THE BOOK OF TOASTS

GLASSWARE

I've always been in two minds when it comes to glassware and champagne. On the one hand, I reckon that fine fizz deserves fine glass. I mean, why spoil things by sipping your 2008 Pol Roger from a Duralex tumbler when it'll taste and look twice as good when sipped from hand-blown, lead crystal from Dartington or Riedel?

On the other hand, if all you've got is a Duralex tumbler, why fret? It's better than nothing. And, if drunk in the right place in the right company on the right occasion – on the sun-dappled bank of a river, say, on a rug with your loved one by your side – your fizz will taste spot-on anyway. And who cares what the heck you drink your fizz out of? Nobody likes a fusspot.

The flute – a tall, slender glass that tapers slightly at the top – is the traditional choice for fizz-lovers. In Hollywood movies they might drink champagne out of coupes – saucer-like glasses on a stem, supposedly modelled originally on the left breast of Marie Antoinette and, more recently on that of Kate Moss, although in La Moss's case I believe it was her right one – but these are usually seen as a bit naff and infra dig.

I've always relied on the Berry Bros & Rudd flute: elegant, dishwasher-safe and fairly priced. Riedel, the family-owned Austrian company founded in 1756, is also many a wine-lover's glassmaker of choice and its wares are indeed exquisite, designed with both science and aesthetics in mind. But the company offers a ridiculous 40 champagne glasses to choose from, including different ones for vintage, non-vintage and rosé champagne (obsessive or what, and where would you store them all?) and also for Prosecco, ranging in price from sensible to silly.

On a recent visit to Dom Pérignon, though, I had a watershed moment. Chef de Cave Richard Geoffroy served his inimitable champagne in large red-wine glasses. In his view, wide-brimmed coupes are too expansive and allow the bubbles to disappear too quickly; flutes are too narrow, making the champagne taste too lean. According to Geoffroy, an ample, red-wine glass makes the champagne taste, well, ample.

We did a bit of a test and tasted some DP – I forget the vintage – out of all three glasses. And blow me, Geoffroy was right. The fizz tasted a lot more expressive, full-flavoured and downright enjoyable out of the red-wine glass.

I've since cleared flutes out of my cupboard entirely, and if anyone raises an eyebrow when I serve them Ridgeview or Bisol or Graham Beck in a red-wine glass, I simply explain that if it's good enough for DP, it's good enough for me and, ergo, my picky guests.

'CHAMPAGNE:
THE GREAT CIVILIZER...'

TALLEYRAND

FRÉDÉRIC GUILBAUD
CHÂTEAU DE LA BRETONNERIE
PERLES DE FOLIE BRUT NV

LOIRE VALLEY, FRANCE

This is something of a curiosity: a sparkling Muscadet. I had never had such a thing before this little charmer was wafted under my beak. Well, to be honest, I had – not that they were *meant* to be fizzy. They were just raw, acidic, badly made, cheap, still Muscadets that had set off some sort of fizzy dirty protest. Either way, they were vile. This, though, is a delight.

The Loire Valley is an exceptionally happy hunting ground for anyone who loves the grape. There is just so much to enjoy there and the wines are just so varied, versatile and tasty. Whites from Sauvignon Blanc (such as Menetou-Salon, Pouilly-Fumé, Quincy and Sancerre) make great apéritifs or partners to first courses; reds from Cabernet Franc (such as Bourgeuil and Chinon) and Pinot Noir (red Sancerre) are ideal for chilling and even serving with fish; and dry, medium or lusciously sweet, food-friendly Chenin Blancs (such as Savennières, Vouvray or Coteaux du Layon) seemingly go with everything. They even make some pretty fine digestifs, too. A large glass of *eau-de-vie de Coing*, anyone?

And of course there are the deliciously accessible sparklers: the Crémants de Loire, the Saumurs and the Vouvrays. Sparkling Muscadet, though, is niche.

Made in the traditional method from 100 per cent Melon de Bourgogne (sometimes known as Muscadet) at his Château de la Bretonnerie estate by Muscadet maestro Frédéric Guilbaud, Perles de Folie is light, dry and crisp, with fresh, zingy apple notes and touches of citrus and warm bread. It makes a great apéritif and, as you might expect given where it comes from, goes brilliantly with oysters and other seafood.

WWW.FREDERICGUILBAUD-VIGNERON.FR

HERBERT HALL BRUT ROSÉ 2014

KENT, ENGLAND

I was introduced to Nick Hall by a mutual friend some ten years ago while researching an article on Plumpton College, the remarkable further education college just north of Brighton, East Sussex. The college specializes in courses such as forestry, agriculture, horticulture, veterinary science and, most interestingly, winemaking and viticulture, the latter two disciplines in which it has built up a formidable international reputation. There are first-class winemakers the world over – from Bordeaux to Barossa – who learned their craft at Plumpton. Nick, then aged 45 and with a thriving art consultancy in London, decided to give it all up to enrol as a student at Plumpton, intent on becoming a winemaker. I'm ashamed to say that I thought he was stark, staring bonkers.

Clearly, I didn't know him very well. The Halls hail from Marden, in the heart of the Kentish Weald, and Nick had seen the hop gardens and orchards of his youth disappear and the distinctive working oast houses turn into second homes for Londoners. Realizing that an empty south-facing slope where his great-grandfather, Herbert Hall, had once farmed would be perfect for the production of quality sparkling wine, Nick – between lectures and practicals at Plumpton – planted 13,000 Chardonnay, Pinot Noir and Pinot Meunier vines and – blow me – ten years later he and his winemaking *confrères* Peter Morgan and Kirsty Smith are making amazingly, jaw-droppingly, tongue-teasingly exquisite wines.

Despite its remarkable success, Herbert Hall remains resolutely artisanal. The winery still looks like a shed and there are no plans to expand the simple 4-hectare organic vineyard. Every bottle is dated and initialled by hand, with the disgorging date written on the back and – I'm not being fanciful – one can feel the love and care that's gone into every bottle.

The 2014 Herbert Hall Brut Rosé is a Kentish jewel. An equal blend of those three grape varieties Nick first planted, it's wonderfully stylish, not only in its beguiling pale-pink colour, but in its creamy mousse and wild strawberry fruit and teasing floral notes on the nose. It's an utter joy.

WWW.HERBERTHALL.COM

CHARLES HEIDSIECK
BRUT RÉSERVE NV

CHAMPAGNE, FRANCE

Charles-Camille Heidsieck (1822–93) was the original
'champagne Charlie', the great-nephew of Florens-Henri
Heidsieck, who, in 1785, founded Heidsieck & Co, which
company later split into the champagne houses we know
today as Heidsieck & Co Monopole and Piper-Heidsieck
(see page 118).

Charles-Camille founded his own eponymous champagne
house in 1851, and was celebrated as one of the first to export
champagne to nineteenth-century America, in famously
vast quantities, and for getting arrested and imprisoned as
a Confederate spy during the American Civil War. He also
had the further posthumous misfortune to be the focus of an
instantly forgettable French-Canadian television film entitled
Champagne Charlie, starring Hugh Grant.

Anyway, the wine that bears Charles Heidsieck's name is an
absolute corker, as fine a non-vintage champagne as you will
find. I had ignored it for years and somehow found myself
being offered a glass of it a year or so ago and was instantly
love-struck.

It's blended from 60 Chardonnay, Pinot Noir and Pinot
Meunier base wines and is crammed full of toasty notes and
those of baked brioche, caramel and white stone fruit. It's
lightly and deliciously honeyed and has a far greater amount
of reserve wines in its blend than almost any of the other major
houses (some 40 per cent, with an average age of ten years)
and is aged for a minimum of six years before release.

It's completely moreish, and I've recommended it
unhesitatingly many times in print. Indeed, only yesterday
I ran into my old chum Peter Grogan, the drinks writer and
rare-book dealer to whom I had mentioned that Charles
Heidsieck Brut Réserve was my current fizz of choice, and
I was thrilled to be told that he now drank nothing else.
How gratifying!

WWW.CHARLESHEIDSIECK.COM

HENRIOT BLANC DE BLANCS NV

CHAMPAGNE, FRANCE

Reims-based champagne Henriot is much admired in the wine trade. Although perhaps not as widely well known as such familiar names as Bollinger, Moët, Veuve Clicquot, Lanson and so on, Henriot has a formidable reputation among those in the know – and rightly so.

The firm has remained in the same family's hands since it was founded in 1808 by Apolline Henriot and includes Burgundy producer Bouchard Père et Fils and Chablis producer William Fèvre in its wider portfolio. Thomas Henriot, son of the late, great Joseph Henriot – sometime head of Veuve Clicquot as well as Champagne Henriot – currently represents the seventh generation.

Henriot is known as a 'Chardonnay house' and is particularly celebrated for the excellence and purity of its fruit. Head winemaker Laurent Fresnet was named Sparkling Winemaker of the Year at the International Wine Challenge in both 2015 and 2016, and in my humble opinion his finest wine is this non-vintage Blanc de Blancs made with fruit grown in the finest villages and vineyard sites in the Côtes de Blanc.

It's surely the best expression of this fine house. There's a fine acidity and an unmistakable minerality to it, but there are also buckets of pure, crisp, clean fruit, too, and hints of honeysuckle, toast and freshly baked pastries on the nose. The blend has a high proportion of reserve wines in it, which only adds to its depth and character.

This Blanc de Blancs is a strikingly fine wine and perfect for those who love champagne made from nothing but the best-quality Chardonnay and no messing about.

WWW.CHAMPAGNE-HENRIOT.COM

INNISKILLIN SPARKLING ICEWINE VIDAL 2014

ONTARIO, CANADA

Think of the world's most celebrated wine regions and I'll bet you a case of fizz that you don't think of Ontario. Yes, *that* Ontario. You know, the one in Canada? Well, they make cracking wines there these days, specifically in the south of the province in the Niagara Peninsula, which lies on the same latitude as northern California to the west and Rome to the east, and which now boasts around 85 wineries.

The summers are bakingly hot and the winters are savagely cold but, thanks to the moderating influence of lakes Ontario and Erie, and the protection of the Niagara Escarpment, the area is ideal for cultivating grapes. You will find crisp Rieslings, soft, characterful Chardonnays, smoky Pinot Noirs and fresh, vibrant Gamays and Cabernet Francs. The finest wines of all, though, are the remarkable Icewines, Canada's greatest gift to the world, thanks to which we might even forgive them for foisting Céline Dion and Justin Bieber upon us all.

Inniskillin, founded in 1975 by Donald Ziraldo and Karl Kaiser, is my favourite producer, and if you thought Icewine was rare, sparkling Icewine is rarer still. This little beauty is made from fully ripe Vidal grapes which are left to freeze on the vine through the winter, long after the conventional harvest is in, to be picked only once the temperature has fallen to below -10°C (14°F). This can be as late as the January or February following the regular vintage. It is extreme winemaking, with grapes picked by hand, one by one, in the most inhospitable conditions, and in minuscule amounts – often as little as five to ten per cent of a normal yield. And if the grapes aren't pressed immediately while still frozen, all is lost.

A tiny amount will then go through the *cuve close* or Charmat process before emerging as a sumptuously, gloriously sweet sparkler like no other. It's ridiculously seductive and perfect with rich starters, fine desserts and blue cheese. Best of all, enjoy it on its own, well chilled, with someone you have designs upon.

WWW.INNISKILLIN.COM

'I AM
A BEER
TEETOTALLER,
NOT A CHAMPAGNE
TEETOTALLER.'

GEORGE BERNARD SHAW

INNOCENT BYSTANDER MOSCATO 2016

VICTORIA, AUSTRALIA

Low-alcohol, sparkling sweet(ish) Moscatos are all the rage in Australia, but none are better than this little gem. It's the market leader, and nothing less than bottled summer. I reckon you would have to have a heart of stone not to enjoy its simple fizzy freshness and grapey exuberance.

The Innocent Bystander winery is noted for its great value Chardonnay, Syrah and Pinot Noir – of which latter wine I've drunk buckets ever since I came across it on my first visit to Victoria – as well as this pink Moscato. Little wonder that nearby Brown Brothers snapped the company up from founder Phil Sexton in early 2016. The new owners have vowed not to change this wine one jot and they'd be mugs if they did, given it is so successful and so downright tasty.

Produced from old vines that line the Murray River in Victoria, it's a blend of 82 per cent Gordo Muscat (aka Muscat of Alexandria) and 18 per cent Black Muscat, a grape that supposedly originated in England in the 1700s and whose parent is probably the famous Black Hamburg vine at Hampton Court. Picked and pressed in the cool of the night, the juice spends just enough time on the grape skins to get this charming pale pink colour. It's then cold-fermented in stainless steel, the process of which is stopped by chilling the wine, leaving it at a very drinkable 5.5%vol.

The resulting wine is just so appealing. It's delectably grapey on the nose (don't laugh… Muscat is the only grape that actually smells of grapes; all the others smell of something else – Cabernet Sauvignon smells like blackcurrant, for example, and Sauvignon Blanc like gooseberry) and fruity in the mouth with watermelon, blackberries, roses and even Turkish Delight on the palate.

I like it best on a hot summer's day, served well chilled with strawberries or raspberries (you can even soak the berries in the wine and a few sprigs of mint to make them a bit more interesting). It's also one of those rare wines that goes really well with chocolate: a notoriously tricky match. It's so tasty and so cheap – go on, give it a go!

WWW.INNOCENTBYSTANDER.COM.AU

JUSTERINI & BROOKS 250TH ANNIVERSARY CHAMPAGNE BRUT NV

CHAMPAGNE, FRANCE

The big champagne houses and famous labels are all very well, but occasionally one stumbles upon an own-label fizz of real style and quality. Most wine merchants and supermarkets boast several on their list and it often pays to give them a whirl. (I feel honour bound to add, though, that it often doesn't.)

This, though, is a little peach. I was sent a bottle by a friend as a thank-you and was instantly smitten. I've since bought several bottles for myself.

Although now owned by drinks giant Diageo, Justerini & Brooks has a venerable history and is as close to a traditional family wine merchant as you can get, trading from fancy offices in London's swanky St. James's Street. The company was founded in 1749 by Giacomo Justerini and George Johnson and began life as Johnson & Justerini. In 1831, one Alfred Brooks took control of the company and changed the name to the one we know today: Justerini & Brooks, a company that has supplied every British monarch since George III.

Anyway, back to this fizz. As J&B approached its 250th anniversary, it was thought fitting to celebrate the milestone with a tip-top own-label champagne. Little did they know how popular it would be and it has been a hardy perennial on their list ever since.

The wine is made for J&B by the small family-run company of Paul Dangin & Fils (talk about family: 11 of them are involved in the company). A blend of Pinot Noir and Pinot Meunier, the grapes are pressed in the traditional manner in a huge vertical press before being gently vinified. The wine then spends at least three years aging on the lees before disgorgement and release.

It's a deliciously rounded and supple wine, generous and toasty, and I love it.

WWW.JUSTERINIS.COM

CUVÉE ESPLENDOR
VARDON KENNETT 2013

CATALONIA, SPAIN

I'd be very surprised if you'd seen this Catalonian sparkler before, so novel is it. In fact, it's so hot off the press that it will only have just beaten this book onto the shelves. I managed to get an early sample, though, so keen was I to try it.

It's made by Spain's leading family-owned producer, Bodegas Torres, which has grown grapes and made wine in Catalonia since the seventeenth century and which is currently headed by fourth-generation Miguel A. Torres.

I lap up pretty much everything the Torres family produces, from cheap-and-cheerful Viña Sol to the swanky, top-of-the-range Grans Muralles with all stations in between. I always look out for the family's Chilean wines (see page 146) and was seduced long ago by the exquisite Pinot Noirs and Chardonnays made by Miguel's sister, Marimar Torres, in California.

Miguel A. Torres and Bodegas Torres have been festooned with awards and accolades, including 'Man of the Year' (*Decanter*), 'Personality of the Year' (*Wine International*), 'Best European Winery of the Year' (*Wine Enthusiast*) and 'Most Important Winery in Spain' (*Wine Spectator*). And in 2017, The Drinks Business named Bodegas Torres 'The World's Most Admired Wine Brand' for the third time. In short, what I'm saying is this: These Guys Know Their Stuff. It's surprising, then, that this is the first traditional method sparkler that Bodegas Torres has produced in Catalonia.

It comes from high-altitude vineyards in the Penedès, 500m above sea level, and is a blend of Pinot Noir (55 per cent), Chardonnay (40 per cent) and the indigenous Xarel-lo (5 per cent). It's part-fermented in oak and spends almost three years on the lees before release.

Named after Daniel Vardon Kennett, the Channel Islander who lived on the estate in the early ninteenth century, it's a real beauty: elegant and feminine, with bracing citrus notes and soothing hints of toast, brioche and freshly baked pastries. There's no question that this is a very fine fizz, well up there with the best that Torres produces.

WWW.TORRES.ES

KLEIN CONSTANTIA
CAP CLASSIQUE BRUT 2012

CONSTANTIA, SOUTH AFRICA

Klein Constantia in the Western Cape is best known for its sublime sweet wine: the Vin de Constance. Many – including myself – would argue that it was one of the finest sweet wines in the world, to be spoken of in the same breath as the mighty Yquem and the finest Tokajis, and I'm chuffed to say that I have a magnum of it biding its time in my so-called cellar (in truth a cobwebbed cupboard under the stairs).

The vineyards were first planted in 1685 by Simon van de Stel, the governor of the Cape, who modestly named Stellenbosch after himself. He had been granted land by the Dutch East India Company and after months of soil and climate analysis chose this as the perfect site for his estate, within a cork's pop of False Bay.

The valley of Constantia is lush and green, thanks to the fact it rains so very much. When I was last there I was buffeted by the most incredible storm and had to take urgent shelter as raindrops the size of gulls' eggs thundered down upon us.

The owner at that time, Lowell Jooste, explained that they had an average annual rainfall of 1.2 metres (4 feet) (it was nearer 2 metres [7 feet] that year) that came over the mountain and just dumped on them. But thanks to the decomposed granite soil draining well, and to having warm, north-facing slopes, perfect altitude and the moderating influence of the ocean, it all added up to having a top spot for growing cool-climate grapes.

Klein Constantia started making sparkling wine – Méthode Cap Classique – in 2005 and quickly won huge praise and many awards for their efforts. I reckon this 2012 is the best yet; it's a remarkably fine wine. Made from 100 per cent Chardonnay, the wine spends nine months in 500-litre barrels before blending and undergoing the second fermentation in bottle. It's fabulously toasty and buttery, but with delicious fresh citrus, too, and even a hint of freshly sliced apples and pears.

So far, each successive vintage of Klein Constantia MCC has been better than the last. It's hard to see, though, how winemaker Matt Day could improve on this little stunner.

WWW.KLEINCONSTANTIA.COM

KLEINE ZALZE BRUT NV

STELLENBOSCH, SOUTH AFRICA

Kleine Zalze is a splendid spot, just a couple of kilometres
south of Stellenbosch, in the heart of South Africa's Western
Cape. Not only can you taste and then buy wine here from
the cellar door, you can eat in the splendid Terroir restaurant;
you can stay in the Cape Dutch-style lodge; you can swim,
hike, cycle, play golf or simply sit beneath the ancient oak
trees and stare at the vines as they lead the eye towards
distant mountains.

In short, the good folk of Kleine Zalze have wine tourism
down to a fine art. They also make first-rate wines. Indeed,
wine has been made in some fashion on the estate since it
was first purchased by Nicholas Cleef in 1695. It wasn't until
exactly 300 years later, though, that the modern Kleine Zalze
was born after the estate was bought by Kobus Basson and
his family.

They make a number of excellent still wines in several different
ranges, from such classic varieties as Sauvignon Blanc, Chenin
Blanc, Cabernet Sauvignon, Shiraz and Pinot Noir. However,
it was only in 2011 that they started making Cap Classique
sparkling wine.

They make a vintage Cap Classique, a Brut Rosé NV and this,
my favourite, the Kleine Zalze Brut NV. A blend of 60 per
cent Chardonnay and 40 per cent Pinot Noir, it's deliciously
stylish and elegant, full of blackberry, strawberry and raspberry
flavours backed by tasty biscuit and brioche notes. It's a fine
apéritif but also weighty enough to match light summer salads,
smoked salmon or simple hot dishes such as seafood pasta.

WWW.KLEINEZALZE.COM

'TO CHAMPAGNE -
A BEVERAGE THAT
MAKES YOU
SEE DOUBLE AND
FEEL SINGLE.'

ANONYMOUS

KRUG GRANDE CUVÉE

CHAMPAGNE, FRANCE

Krug is unique. It might be just one of the many champagne houses owned by Louis Vuitton-Moët Hennessy (along with Moët itself, Dom Pérignon, Veuve Clicquot, Mercier and Ruinart), but there's nothing else quite like it.

The house was founded in 1843 by Joseph Krug, and despite its purchase by LVMH in 1999, the Krug family is still closely involved in its running. Olivier Krug, son of Henri and nephew of Rémi, currently represents the sixth generation.

I have a bottle of Krug Grande Cuvée in front of me as I write. It's what I might laughingly term Krug's entry-level wine. I say laughingly because it's just shy of £130 (US$170) a bottle and is the quality of most other house's *prestige cuvées*. There's a six-figure ID number on the back label, unique to every bottle.

I type said code into a box on the Krug website (apparently I could scan the bottle with some app or other or use my phone if I knew how to do such things) and the following information comes up: it's made from 37 per cent Pinot Noir, 32 per cent Chardonnay and 31 per cent Pinot Meunier, blended from 183 different wines from twelve different years, the oldest being from 1990 and the youngest from 2007; the latter year comprises 73 per cent of the blend. It spent nine years maturing on the lees in the cellars and was bottled in the winter of 2015/16. Finally, I learn that this bottle is the 163rd edition, that's to say it's the 163rd release of Krug's Grande Cuvée since the house's foundation.

Now that's what I call being given the lowdown.

The wine itself is extraordinarily complex, displaying power and finesse, richness and subtlety, ripeness and freshness – all of which are usually contrary attributes. It's delicately honeyed, with rounded notes of toast and brioche, dried fruit and fresh citrus and a thousand things besides. The finish just goes on and on and on.

Krug is the only house that has offered a different *cuvée* every year for 163 years, a sort of multi-vintage for the connoisseur and nobody has copied it. As I say, Krug is unique.

WWW.KRUG.COM

LANGLOIS-CHATEAU
CRÉMANT DE LOIRE BRUT NV

LOIRE VALLEY, FRANCE

I'm ashamed to say that I've only been to the medieval town of Saumur in the Loire Valley just once, although I'll never forget my visit. It wasn't so much the absurdly varied drinks I drank during my 36 hours there, but more the titanic quantities in which I drank them.

I started at Langlois-Chateau (spelt without the circumflex, since *Chateau* in this instance is the name of its co-founder – Jeanne Chateau – rather the French word for castle), producer of fine wines since 1885, and ended, via several liquid diversions, just down the road at the Combier Distillery, producer of fine spirits since 1834. I drank far too much at both (and in between) and although there were spittoons on offer at the former, I didn't make as much use of them as I should have. Unfortunately, there were no spittoons at all on offer at the latter, but by then it was already too late. If I tell you that I finished my tasting at Combier with a selection of five absinthes, I'm sure you will understand how it was that the wheels finally came off my wagon. It's fair to say that I left in some disarray.

I digress. I've always been a huge fan of Langlois-Chateau's fizzes. My father always had some in his fridge and I sampled them at an early age. They make a number of wines here, both still and sparkling, but the one for which Langlois-Chateau is best known is this smooth, honeyed sparkler made in the traditional method from an intriguing blend of hand-picked Chenin Blanc (60 per cent), Chardonnay (20 per cent) and Cabernet Franc (20 per cent) and aged for two years on the lees.

The Loire Valley is France's second-largest region for sparkling wine, so there's no shortage of expertise about. Add to this the fact that Langlois-Chateau has been largely owned by the Bollinger family since 1973 and you get a bit of Champenois expertise and stardust in the mix, too.

It's a cracking fizz this – full of peaches, pears and quinces – and wonderfully well priced. It's my 'go-to' fizz on many an occasion.

WWW.LANGLOIS-CHATEAU.FR

CHAMPAGNE SWEETNESS LEVELS

We all have our favourite fizz. It might be a particular house style that appeals to us, the glamour of a particular brand or simply how dry or sweet a particular wine might be.

Most traditional method champagnes and sparkling wines are described as brut – that's to say, dry. But this is only part of a very confusing story, because one brand's dry is another brand's, well, not quite so dry or possibly even drier. It's all to do with how much sugar is added.

In order to counterbalance the acidity in any given traditional method sparkler, a mixture of wine and cane sugar solution known as *liqueur d'expédition* is introduced to the bottle immediately prior to corking and labelling. The amount of sugar in this solution is known as the dosage, and it is this that determines a traditional method sparkler's sweetness level.

In the past, champagne used to be much sweeter than we are accustomed to nowadays, especially at the turn of the last century, and it is only really since the 1920s that drier styles have taken over. Today, there is a distinct vogue for bone-dry fizzes with no dosage at all, whatever sweetness there might be in the wine coming from the fruit rather than from added sugar.

In the Champagne region, where grapes sometimes struggle to ripen, this can mean that the wines are searingly dry. In Franciacorta, in Italy, say, they consider the zero-dosage wines more palatable because they get riper fruit, thanks to the warmer climate. There is therefore less need to sweeten the wines with sugar.

One might imagine that those champagnes called extra dry would be just that, but actually they are not as dry as either brut or brut extra, having up to 20 grams of residual sugar per litre. *Sec* (meaning dry) champagne isn't really dry at all, with between 20 and 35 grams, while demi-sec has between 35 and 50 grams and 'rich' has over 50 grams.

And within each category, each brand is different. Bollinger Special Cuvée Brut, for example, has a dosage of between 8 and 9 grams of residual sugar per litre; Pol Roger Brut Reserve has 9 grams; Veuve Clicquot Yellow Label has 10 grams and Louis Roederer Brut Premier has 11 to 12 grams. Even more confusing is the fact that, for example, Pol Roger's Demi-Sec calls itself 'rich', whereas Veuve Clicquot's Demi-Sec doesn't, although its Rich Reserve calls itself *sec*. Baffling!

So, just for the record, here are the terms you are likely to see on the labels of champagne and many other traditional method sparklers and their approximate sugar levels:

BRUT SAUVAGE, BRUT NATURE, BRUT ZÉRO, ULTRA BRUT:
bone dry (0–3 grams per litre/gpl of residual sugar)

BRUT EXTRA, EXTRA BRUT:
very dry to dry (0–6 gpl)

BRUT:
dry (6–12 gpl)

EXTRA DRY, EXTRA SEC.
dry to medium dry (12–20 gpl)

SEC, DRY:
medium to medium-sweet (20–35 gpl)

DEMI-SEC:
medium-sweet to sweet (35–50 gpl)

RICH, DOUX:
sweet to very sweet (50+ gpl)

LAURENT-PERRIER DEMI-SEC NV

CHAMPAGNE, FRANCE

I've lost count of the number of weddings I've attended where slices of cake are handed round, glasses are charged with champagne and we toast the happy couple – immediately after which there's a general wince and grimace around the room. This is never any reflection on our good wishes for the freshly minted Mr & Mrs, you understand; it's simply the unpleasant effect on our collective palate of sweet wedding cake and dry champagne. Future couples please note: the combo just does not work. What you need is a so-called demi-sec or sweet champagne.

Our grandparents and great-grandparents were used to much sweeter champagnes and it was only around 100 years ago that drier styles became more fashionable. Nowadays, of course, there are some champagnes that are drier than ever, with a vogue for ultra brut, brut zero, zero dosage or whatever it is each house chooses to call them.

Put simply, sweet champagne is dry champagne with added sugar. For more on the dosage that determines a champagne's sweetness level, see page 92.

Laurent-Perrier, founded in 1812, and famous for its superb rosé champagne makes a very fine Ultra Brut with no added sugar. Its regular Brut Champagne has a dosage of 10 grams per litre, whereas this sweeter sibling, the Demi-Sec, has one of 40 grams per litre.

Yes, yes, I know. This sounds ridiculously sweet, but it isn't; it's just gorgeous. Indeed, when drunk with wedding cake, it doesn't taste sweet at all, it just tastes *right*. It's also perfect with rich starters such as smoked eel or foie gras, and it's great with salty cheeses and wonderful with dessert.

For my money, though, it's best enjoyed on its own, as an 11A.M. kick-starter, a tricky time of day for the wine-lover when a regular fizz – and especially an ultra-dry one – is just too much of an aggressive assault on one's system.

WWW.LAURENT-PERRIER.COM

PETER LEHMANN BLACK QUEEN SPARKLING SHIRAZ 2011

BAROSSA VALLEY, AUSTRALIA

I've always been a bit wary of sparkling red wines (or should that be red sparkling wines?). Sweet Lambrusco of sainted '70s memory is one thing (see page 52) – but a dry sparkling Shiraz from Australia? It just doesn't seem right. Or rather it *didn't* seem right because, of course, I've since seen the light.

I first came across this fizzy Shiraz at the Terrace Hotel in Perth, Western Australia. When I had last visited Perth more than ten years previously, it had been well and truly shut, with nobody around, nothing to see and nothing to do. I was bored to screams and couldn't wait to leave. Now, though, the place was buzzing, with fabulous bars, hotels and restaurants. It was a city transformed and I loved it.

The Terrace Hotel had only just opened and I was drawn there by its already-famous wine list which ran to what seemed like hundreds of pages. Being in Western Australia I had almost drunk my fill of Margaret River wines (if it's possible to do such a thing, so fine are they) and asked the sommelier to suggest something a little bit different. He came up with this.

Made from 100 per cent Shiraz (what Europeans call Syrah) from the Barossa Valley, it's based on a style of Aussie wine that was first produced in the late nineteenth century and was known as 'sparkling burgundy'. It's fermented on its skins, aged for a year in old oak hogsheads, then bottle-fermented and aged on the lees for two years before release.

It's dry but richly flavoured, with mulberries, loganberries, cherries, vanilla and liquorice all in the mix before it ends with a long, savoury finish. It's different, all right, and really rather wonderful.

Being half-Australian, my wife, Marina, loves it. But then, being also half-Scottish, she drinks just about anything, so long as whatever it is she's drinking is no less than 13%vol. This is 14%vol, so well within her parameters, and she reckons it's absolutely spot-on at brunch, after the Bloody Mary and before the coffee, alongside plates groaning with sausages, eggs, bacon and black pudding. See what you think.

WWW.PETERLEHMANNWINES.COM

CHAMPAGNE ALBERT LEVASSEUR RUE DE SORBIER BRUT NV

CHAMPAGNE, FRANCE

This is a tremendous champagne and, unlike any of the other fizzes within these pages, it's one that's made largely from Pinot Meunier, a grape that's more used to making up the numbers than taking star billing.

Champagne Albert Levasseur was established during the Second World War in the tiny village of Cuchery, some 15km (9 miles) northwest of Épernay. It has been run since 2003 by David Levasseur, grandson of founder Albert.

David, who's something of a philosopher-poet-winemaker, calls himself an Awakener of Senses. He farms his 4.2 hectares, spread over 18 different plots, organically, and he uses only his own fruit. It's a tiny enterprise – he produces no more than 3,000 cases a year – and everything is done by hand.

There's an excellent demi-sec in the Rue du Sorbier range (which is named after the street in which the winery and David's home sit), a brut nature and this, the straightforward brut. He also does a vintage and the wonderful Blanc de Terroir Extra Brut, made from just Chardonnay, and the Noir de Terroir Brut, made from just Pinot Noir. The bottles are sealed in a very artisanal, retro fashion by string and sealing wax.

David also makes Ratafia de Champagne – the traditional liqueur of the region – which I've not tried but which I'm told is also stupendously delicious.

This Rue de Sorbier Brut, though, is more than good enough for me. A blend of 80 per cent Pinot Meunier, 15 per cent Pinot Noir and 5 per cent Chardonnay, it's fabulously fruity, with peaches and pears to the fore and plums and redcurrants and even a touch of spice lurking tastily in the background. There's a vibrant freshness to the fizz, too, and the overall effect is that of something that really speaks of where it's from and the love with which it was made.

WWW.CHAMPAGNE-LEVASSEUR.FR

DOMAINE DE L'IDYLLE
PÉTILLE IDYLLE
CRÉMANT DE SAVOIE NV

SAVOIE, FRANCE

The Tiollier family has been making wine in Savoie in the far east of France since 1840, and their 47 hectares of vineyards are not so much in the foothills of the Alps as in the Alps themselves. This is mountain country and no mistake.

Sparkling wines are a big bit of what *la famille* Tiollier do and they've made them for ages, although it was only in 2015 that Savoie joined Alsace, Bourgogne, Bordeaux, Die, Jura, Limoux and Loire as the eighth region in the list of official crémant *appellations*.

The Tiollier fizz is made in the traditional manner from the local Jacquère grape – a delicately perfumed, high-yielding variety originally introduced to the region by the monks at Chartreuse and found hardly anywhere else – plus a splash of Altesse, aka Roussette.

One doesn't often see wines such as this exported; it's usually drunk *en plein air* by thirsty skiers after a black run or two. I'm indebted to my old chum Jason Yapp, of West Country wine merchants Yapp Bros, who ran this to ground a year or so back, vinous truffle-hound that he is, and who has been raving about it ever since.

It's something of a hard sell, it's true, and not something you will find in a supermarket. The complete lack of any information at all on the front label as to how it's made and what from, and with no back label to speak of doesn't exactly help its cause.

But it is indeed a charmer: light, fruity, zesty, creamy and undemanding – a veritable breath of mountain air, clean and fresh as a snowflake.

WWW.VIN-SAVOIE-IDYLLE.FR

LINDAUER SPECIAL RESERVE BRUT CUVÉE NV

HAWKE'S BAY/GISBORNE, NEW ZEALAND

I've always really enjoyed the Lindaeur sparklers from New Zealand, and although there are at least 12 different *cuvées* in the range, unfortunately the only one you can get your hands on in the UK these days is this Lindauer Special Reserve Brut Cuvée.

Happily, it's my favourite, just because it's so darn, well, drinkable. It's about as perfect a party wine as you'll find and always ridiculously good value. Although the retail price is supposedly £13 (US$17), at the time of writing, when I last looked you could pick up a bottle for nearly half the price in my local wine shop, so long as you bought it as part of a mixed half-dozen.

And to be honest, I don't know how the heck they can knock it out so cheaply. After all, it's a bottle-fermented fizz of some pedigree, blended from 60 per cent Pinot Noir and 40 per cent Chardonnay grown in both Hawke's Bay and Gisborne. It's fresh, it's frivolous and it's fab.

Apparently the brand, which launched in 1981 and is owned by Lion, New Zealand's largest drinks firm, was named after the painter Gottfried Lindauer (1839–1926), a Czech artist who made his name painting the Maori.

I've seen Lindauer's marketing blurb and it makes no bones about the fact that the fizz is aimed squarely at 27- to 33-year-old outgoing females. Feminine and stylish, moderately aspirational with a touch of worldliness, looking to have effortless fun occasions with friends. Well, hark at them being all sexist. Boys like to have fun, too, you know.

I can't imagine Krug, Bollinger or Pol Roger coming up with guff, but so what? Lindauer is far and away New Zealand's best-selling fizz, and all power to it because it's bloody good.

WWW.LINDAUER.CO.NZ

CAVE DE LUGNY BRUT MILLÉSIMÉ CRÉMANT DE BOURGOGNE 2013

BURGUNDY, FRANCE

We have served this little gem at several *Spectator* Wine Club lunches recently and featured it at the *Spectator* Wine School where it never fails to stop folk in their tracks. Three questions inevitably follow: What the heck is this fabulous fizz? How much is it? Where can I get some? The answers: a traditional method sparkler from the Cave de Lugny cooperative in Burgundy; £14.95 (US$20); from www.fromvineyardsdirect. com or www.winesearcher.com.

I simply love it and drink it whenever I get the chance. I mean, it is ridiculously cheap for what it is, but it looks and tastes really fine. And I don't care what you say: looks are important. If the bottle looks impressive you're likely to be impressed and to be well disposed to the wine before you even taste it. This bottle wouldn't look out of place on a shelf of champagnes. It looks seriously good – and it is.

Only the first-press juice of top-quality, hand-picked Chardonnay and Pinot Noir, grown on clay/limestone soil around Lugny, in the heart of Burgundy's Mâconnais area, is used, after which it undergoes cool fermentation in steel tanks. A tiny proportion of the Chardonnay is then aged in oak before blending with the rest of the cuvée. The blend is then aged for 18 months before release, and is about as fine a fizz as you can find with loose change.

It has depth, weight, character and real panache, with hints of peaches and cream, nuts, and toasted brioche. I would be amazed if you didn't absolutely love it.

WWW.CAVE-LUGNY.COM

SERGE MATHIEU
BRUT TRADITION NV

CHAMPAGNE, FRANCE

I first tasted this with a friend who was raving about this wonderful fizz he'd found during a weekend in Champagne and couldn't wait to show to me. Did I fancy popping over?

This happens a fair bit. Wine-loving mates can't wait to show off their latest obscure vinous discovery found on holiday, and I dread having to lie about how great it is while simultaneously trying to find some pot plant in which to pour the rest of the glass. The last wine Andrew showed me was a blue – yes, *blue* – Chardonnay from Spain.

On this occasion I toddled over, fully expecting the ritual to be repeated, only to find that I was stopped completely in my tracks by my very first sip. Serge Mathieu Brut Tradition was clearly an absolutely top-notch champagne. Andrew couldn't stop grinning. I couldn't stop drinking.

I blush, really blush, to admit that I had never heard of it. So much for me being a so-called expert. Ignorant fool, more like. And worst of all, every friend in the trade and wine press I mentioned Serge Mathieu to knew all about him and his wines. 'Oh yes, I adore them!'

Of course, I've since seen Serge Mathieu's champagnes on all sorts of wine lists, not least that of www.fromvineyardsdirect. com. FVD's Esme Johnstone has been a fan ever since he discovered them in a wine bar in Paris. I'm smitten, too.

A small producer in Avirey-Lingey, Serge Mathieu is the sixth generation of his family to grow grapes (they started in 1760), and his daughter, Isabelle, is the seventh. She and her husband Michel now run the enterprise, the vineyards farmed sustainably and as biodynamically as the local climate will allow. They even use horses for ploughing between the vines.

The Brut Tradition is 100 per cent Pinot Noir and is aged for four years on the lees. It's mouth-fillingly fine, with plenty of luscious, creamy, red-fruit flavours, a whisper of honey on the nose and a finish that goes on forever. It's half the price of many a more famous champagne and just as fine.

WWW.CHAMPAGNE-SERGE-MATHIEU.FR

'HE WHO
DOESN'T RISK
NEVER GETS
TO DRINK
CHAMPAGNE.'

RUSSIAN PROVERB

MIOLO MILLÉSIME ESPUMANTE BRUT 2012

VALE DOS VINHEDOS, BRAZIL

As we all know, Brazil's greatest gift to the world is its wonderful cachaça. Well, cachaça and Gisele Bündchen. Served as a caipirinha and mixed with one whole lime cut into eighths and muddled with plenty of sugar and ice, the fermented and distilled sugar-cane juice that is cachaça becomes one of the most uplifting of all drinks.

You can ring the changes by mixing cachaça with orange juice and fresh grated ginger; with watermelon juice and even with coconut milk. All versions are spectacularly tasty and I drink little else when in Brazil. Except I've now discovered Brazilian wine.

And it was a bottle of Miolo Brut Millésime, a traditional method sparkling wine made from Chardonnay and Pinot Noir, that first stopped me in my tracks. Like the current vintage – the 2012 – it was crisp, toasty and faintly honeyed and utterly delicious. Brazil is already the sixteenth-largest wine producer in the world, but it still came as a surprise to taste wine of this quality.

Founded in 1897 simply to grow grapes, Miolo started making wine around thirty years ago and is now the biggest wine company in the country, in the hands of the family's fourth generation. It boasts 1,200 hectares under vine across six regions in Brazil, exports to 25 countries and boasts the legendary Michel Rolland as consultant. Its sparkler (one of many in its portfolio) comes from the far south of the country, in the appropriately named Vale dos Vinhedos (Valley of Vineyards), not far from Porto Alegre.

This lush, green valley was settled by wine-loving Italian immigrants in the nineteenth century, and most of the wineries remain family owned. Of the wines made here, the Merlot-, Cabernet- and Tannat-based reds and Chardonnay whites really aren't bad at all, but it is the sparkling wines that truly stand out.

The Miolo Brut Millésime is hugely impressive, and I've had great fun of late offering it to friends and asking them to guess where it's from. I'm happy to say that nobody has ever yet said Brazil. One day they will, for the wines are just getting better. After all, it wasn't so long ago that folk scoffed at the idea of Chile and Argentina ever making anything palatable.

WWW.MIOLO.COM.BR

'GENTLEMEN, IN THE LITTLE MOMENT THAT REMAINS TO US BETWEEN THE CRISIS AND THE CATASTROPHE, WE MAY AS WELL DRINK A GLASS OF CHAMPAGNE.'

PAUL CLAUDEL

MOËT & CHANDON BRUT IMPÉRIAL NV

CHAMPAGNE, FRANCE

Not only does Moët & Chandon produce more champagne than anybody else, but its Brut Impérial is also the world's best-selling champagne by several miles. And although the powers-that-be are annoyingly coy about revealing even the roughest of production figures, they do admit to Moët being the biggest vineyard-owner in Champagne, boasting some 1,000 hectares (Veuve Clicquot, the second biggest, has 500) and to buying in the fruit from a further 2,500 hectares.

Oh, and it's Moët with a hard 't' by the way, the house's founder, Claude Moët, being of Dutch heritage. So it's *Mo-wett* to rhyme with 'poet', rather than *Mo-way* to rhyme with 'no way'. Which is a shame, as it rather ruins one of my favourite tales, that of the apocryphal music act (I've heard it attributed to Led Zeppelin, DJ Carl Cox, Terrorvision, Nina Simone and even Spinal Tap), whose rider at gigs was to have plenty of champagne *en magnum* in the green room. As the tour manager apparently insisted: 'No Mo-way, no show-ay; no Chandon, no band on.'

Jean-Rémy Moët, the pioneering spirit of the company and grandson of the founder, was a friend of Napoléon Bonaparte. The two men were at military academy together and in the labyrinthine cellars cut deep into the chalk beneath Moët's offices in Épernay (the cellars stretch for over 27km [17 miles], making them the largest in the region) there stands a well-lit and handsomely carved wooden barrel. A plaque records that the barrel was given to Jean-Rémy in 1810 by Napoléon after the latter had nicked it – full of Port – from the King of Bavaria, who himself had been given it by the King of Portugal.

Napoléon visited Moët & Chandon on many occasions and decorated Jean-Rémy with the Légion d'Honneur here, and it is to commemorate this friendship that Moët calls its non-vintage Champagne Brut Impérial.

The thing is, despite the massive amounts produced, it's still so good. It used to be a bit uncool to admit to liking Moët, but Chef de Cave Benoît Gouez is an extremely skilled winemaker. I'm out and proud as a huge fan of his fizz.

WWW.MOET.COM

MOËT & CHANDON
ICE IMPÉRIAL NV

CHAMPAGNE, FRANCE

When compiling my list of fizzes for this book, I promised myself that I would only have one example from each producer and that I'd spread things out a bit.

I hope you will forgive me, then, for breaking my own rule, if only because this Moët & Chandon Ice Impérial NV is almost a completely different product from its near namesake, the Moët & Chandon Brut Impérial NV. At least, it's meant to be enjoyed in a very different way.

The purists will hate it, of course, and will dismiss it simply as an empty marketing wheeze, whereas I would argue that it shows that Moët is moving sensibly with the times and making its wines as accessible as possible to a new generation of potential champagne drinkers. With the likes of Prosecco and Moscato d'Asti enjoying rocketing sales among the younger drinking generation, champagne producers need to appeal to as wide an audience as possible or risk losing sales to such other sparklers for good.

And so it is that Moët has come up with this rather fabulous fizz that's designed specifically to be drunk over ice. Yep, that's to say in a glass *with ice cubes floating around in it.* There: I said you'd hate it! Look, I wouldn't want to drink my Dom Pérignon like this nor my Krug Grande Cuvée, nor even my Ca'del Bosco Franciacorta. But somehow this just works. Moët's chef de cave, Benoît Gouez, noticed the recent trend for folk to drink their champagne on ice (a drink known as a *piscine* in France) and feared this would ruin the balance of the brut champagnes they were knocking back. He therefore created this special demi-sec.

Dominated by Pinot Noir (which comprises up to 50 per cent of the blend) and Pinot Meunier (up to 40 per cent) with just 10 per cent Chardonnay, it has a socking great dosage of 45 grams per litre of sugar. This, according to Gouez, is the key, for it gives the wine its structure and helps maintain the balance between fizz and ice. The best way to drink it is in a large wine glass with three sizeable ice cubes. I dare you to try it.

WWW.MOET.COM

MONTE ROSSA CABOCHON FRANCIACORTA BRUT 2011

FRANCIACORTA, ITALY

Monte Rossa is one of the longer-established producers of Franciacorta in Italy, having been founded in 1972 by entrepreneur Paolo Rabotti and his wife, Paola. And it's a beautiful spot, too, with its elegant sixteenth-century villa, cypress trees and rolling vineyards.

Paolo and Paola's son, Emanuele Rabotti, is currently in charge. Having made still wines since the very beginning, he now concentrates on just making sparkling wines, and Monte Rossa currently produces some 500,000 bottles a year.

Cabochon is the top of the company's range, first produced in 1985 from the finest vineyards of the hill of Monte Rossa itself. A blend of 70 per cent hand-harvested Chardonnay and 30 per cent hand-harvested Pinot Nero, the wine is fermented first in oak *barriques*, giving great depth of flavour and a rounded palate and is made by the so-called *saignée* method, whereby the fermenting juice is taken off the grape skins before it takes on too much colour, leaving it a delicate shade of pink. After three years on the lees, even greater complexity develops with hints of apricot, pineapple, papaya, toast, pastry and brioche emerging on the palate. It's dry but succulent, with feather-light bubbles and a wonderfully long finish.

If you have yet to discover the fabulous fizzes of Franciacorta, you are in for an effervescent, eye-opening, tongue-tingling treat. If you know them already, you will completely understand why I am so smitten with them.

WWW.MONTEROSSA.COM

MUMM GRAND CORDON BRUT NV

CHAMPAGNE, FRANCE

I renewed my fondness for the champagnes of G.H. Mumm
a few years ago. This was after spending the day with Chef de
Cave Didier Mariotti as he selected the final wines for the latest
batch of Mumm Cordon Rouge, the non-vintage blend that
accounts for 85 per cent of the company's volume.

Didier explained how he and his team had whittled down an
original selection of 300 recently fermented wines – drawn from
eighty or so different *crus* (hundreds of vineyards and blocks
within vineyards) – to the fifty that faced us that day. I found
them almost unpalatable, as they were so young, raw and acidic,
but I was fascinated to see how Didier wove them all together
into something that would ultimately be deliciously drinkable.

During the late eighties and nineties, Mumm was notorious
for the underwhelming quality of its wines. The once-assured
producer was deep in the doldrums as its owner, Seagram,
lost interest before finally offloading it in order to buy a
film company. After passing through various hands, Mumm
finally ended up with drinks giant Pernod Ricard. It poached
Mariotti from the Nicolas Feuillatte cooperative and instructed
him to build on his immediate predecessor's success in
improving quality.

Today Mumm is in rude health. The company remains a big
player – the third-largest producer behind Moët & Chandon
and Veuve Clicquot – but with quality vastly improved and the
wines are a real pleasure to quaff.

Mumm's marketing is cool, trendy and witty, too. It's heavily
sport-orientated (think Formula 1) and the company has
recently had great fun appointing sprinter Usain Bolt as its
new CEO (chief entertainment officer).

Most striking of all has been the recent launch of Mumm
Grand Cordon Brut NV. As the successor to the fabled Cordon
Rouge, the bottle retains the red ribbon across its front, but
this time it's cleverly indented into the glass of the wonderfully
stylish, label-free bottle. And the wine's an absolute peach. A
blend of 45 per cent Pinot Noir, 30 per cent Chardonnay and
25 per cent Pinot Meunier, it has weight and power, elegance
and finesse and more than lives up to the beauty of its bottle.

WWW.MUMM.COM

NARRATIVE ANCIENT METHOD
BY OKANAGAN CRUSH PAD 2013

BRITISH COLUMBIA, CANADA

Well, to be honest, I really didn't know what to make of this
when I first stumbled across it: a bizarrely named Canadian fizz
in a plain green bottle with a basic, let's-not-give-much-away
front label, no neck foil, a simple crown cap for a stopper and a
fairly big price tag. I mean, what the heck's all that about?

It turns out the bottle came from Summerland in British
Columbia's Okanagan Valley, some 400km (250 miles) east of
Vancouver. And it was here, in 2011, that Christine Coletta
and Steve Lornie founded the Okanagan Crush Pad winery at
Switchback Organic Vineyard, partly as a place for the two of
them and winemaker Matt Dumayne to make their own organic
and biodynamic wines (under their Haywire and Narrative
labels), but also for local small growers and winemakers without
facilities and equipment of their own to do likewise.

This Narrative fizz is made from 100 per cent Chardonnay
using the so-called ancient or ancestral method, sometimes
known as the *méthode ancestrale* or *pétillant naturel* (or *pét-nat*),
whereby the initial fermentation continues in the bottle without
any filtering, fining or stabilizing taking place. This is how
Blanquette de Limoux in the Languedoc is made.

It's a wine unlike any other, from a unique and strange wine
region that I'm told has both deserts and snow, using a rare
and ancient method of production. It has a honeyed citrus and
toasty scent, and intense, concentrated, ripe- and baked-apple
flavours, a touch of citrus again plus something comforting and
warm – hay, maybe – along with brown bread and brioche. It's
a true and amazing one-off – sadly with a price tag to match.

WWW.OKANAGANCRUSHPAD.COM

NO. 1 FAMILY ESTATE ASSEMBLÉ NV

MARLBOROUGH, NEW ZEALAND

If any New Zealand fizz has pedigree, it's this one from Daniel le Brun, a Frenchman by birth (born in Champagne no less) and a New Zealander by adoption. But don't be confused: the winery that bears Daniel le Brun's name – and which he founded in 1980 – is now owned by the Antipodean drinks giant Lion Nathan, D le B having lost control of the company to a former business partner in 1996. Three years later, though, le Brun was back with his new enterprise, No. 1 Family Estate, based in Rapaura, a small village just outside Blenheim in Marlborough.

And as the scion of an ancient champagne-making family (he's the twelfth generation to make fizz), le Brun concentrates on making sparkling wine and nothing but. Needless to say, the wines are produced by the traditional method, although le Brun has started unilaterally to label his wines 'Méthode Marlborough', which he and his family hope will become the standard term for sparkling wines made within the region.

The criteria are simple: the wine must be made exclusively from Marlborough-grown Chardonnay, Pinot Noir and Pinot Meunier (blended or singly); the wine must undergo a secondary fermentation in bottle *à la méthode traditionelle*, and it must spend at least 18 months on the lees before disgorging.

There are six wines in the No. 1 Family Estate range and this, the entry-level fizz, is my favourite. It's just so crisp, clean and appealing. Being so light, delicate and fresh, it makes a wonderful apéritif and is the perfect combination of Daniel le Brun's Champenois heritage and Kiwi can-do attitude.

WWW.NO1FAMILYESTATE.CO.NZ

NYETIMBER TILLINGTON SINGLE VINEYARD 2010

WEST SUSSEX, ENGLAND

You can't claim to know or understand English sparkling wine until you've tried something from Nyetimber. It wasn't the first producer of English fizz, nor is it necessarily the best, but it's certainly the best known and most lauded.

Nyetimber has a noble history. Lying near Pulborough, in West Sussex, the estate was given by a grateful William the Conqueror to Earl Godwin in 1086. It later belonged variously to Earl de la Warenne, the Cluniac Priory of Lewes, Thomas Cromwell and Henry VIII's fourth wife, Anne of Cleves.

Fast-forward to 1987, the year the estate was bought by Stuart and Sandy Moss from Chicago. Stuart was a wealthy manufacturer of medical and dental equipment and Sandy was a successful antique dealer and archaeologist. They fell in love with the beautiful medieval house and decided to make it their home. They also decided to grow vines and make wine. The Mosses had never made wine before, but having determined that both soil and climate were ideal, and having decided to plant the three classic champagne varieties – the first to do so in England – they never looked back. Their wines were festooned with awards and plaudits and there is no question that without Nyetimber making such a success of things, other English sparkling wines following in its wake would not have had the reception they have had.

The Mosses sold the estate to songwriter Andy Hill, and he sold it to Dutch squillionaire Eric Heerema. Mr Heerema might find it difficult to hold on to staff and he might notoriously have put the Savoy Hotel's nose out of joint (no room to explain here: Google the story if it you want), but in Cherie Spriggs he has an exceptional winemaker, and her wines are stunning.

The icing on Nyetimber's cake is the remarkable 2010 Tillington Single Vineyard. Made from a blend of 78 per cent Pinot Noir and 22 per cent Chardonnay it's the first single-vineyard English fizz, and only 4,117 individually numbered bottles were made. It's pale, pale gold in colour with fresh, ripe red fruit on nose and palate and a long, toasty, nutty finish. It's an amazing wine.

WWW.NYETIMBER.COM

BRUNO PAILLARD
NEC PLUS ULTRA 2002

CHAMPAGNE, FRANCE

Bruno Paillard is one of the new kids on the champagne block, the house that bears his name having only been founded as recently as 1981 and – the 27-year-old Bruno not having a dime to his name at the time – funded by the sale of his precious vintage Jaguar car. BP didn't own any vineyards until 1994, but he now has 32 hectares and buys in the rest of the fruit he needs from the small growers he has used since the very beginning.

Champagne Bruno Paillard, which Bruno now co-manages with his daughter, Alice, has six fizzes in its range, starting with a very tasty Brut Première Cuvée and ending with this fabulous barrel-fermented *prestige cuvée*, the Bruno Paillard Nec Plus Ultra ('The Ultimate').

The 2002 is only the sixth vintage of this wine to be released, and only 6,200 bottles were produced, each one individually numbered. It's rare and precious stuff, for sure – Bruno Paillard's attempt to make the greatest-possible champagne – and as prized by wine-lovers as it is by collectors. Don't be too baffled if you've already seen the 2003 vintage knocking about; it matured earlier than the 2002 and so was released earlier. This leap-frogging of vintages happens surprisingly often in champagne, and shows just how capricious the wines are: not unlike maturing (or – more likely – non-maturing) teenage children.

A half-and-half blend of Pinot Noir and Chardonnay, it's a big, bold wine yet also commendably accessible. It's complex all right, but the fresh, ripe fruit and deeper honey-and-nut flavours shine through and throw their arms around you in a glorious fizzy embrace. It's for nights at the opera or special birthdays rather than a quick swig en route to dinner – and none the worse for being so.

WWW.CHAMPAGNEBRUNOPAILLARD.COM

'COME QUICKLY, I AM TASTING THE STARS!'

DOM PÉRIGNON

FIZZ AND FOOD

OK, settle down at the back. Quiet, please. Hands up who last drank fizz during a meal? Hmm, not many; hardly any of you in fact. And I'm not in the least surprised. After all, it's not really what we do, is it? It's not what fizz is for.

I mean, we're more than happy to have a cheeky Prosecco with friends on the way home after work and maybe a glass of champagne on our birthday or as an apéritif before a fine dinner. And we'll almost certainly sink a Buck's Fizz or four at a wedding. But bubbles with a meal? Erm, thanks, but no thanks.

But it wasn't always like that and nor should it be today. Before the Second World War, it wasn't unknown for champagne houses to lob a slug of brandy into their wines along with the regular dosage of sugar, as a result of which the fizz of the 1920s and 1930s was big and hefty and invariably consumed throughout a meal. It was quite normal for the fine-dining classes back then to have a dry martini, say, or sherry before the meal, fizz throughout the first and the main courses, Bordeaux or Burgundy with the savoury, and dessert wine or Port with the dessert. It was only in the 1950s, with the emergence of lighter, more Chardonnay-influenced non-vintage champagnes (prior to this champagne was vintage wine only), that fizz came to be drunk more as an apéritif and less as a partner to grub.

I reckon it's time to redress the balance and to get used to drinking champagne and fine sparklers with a meal. Not necessarily all the way through the meal, mind, nor even every day – just this course and that and just now and then. After all, champagne deserves more than simply to be the curtain-raiser to a fine feast. It should be part of the show itself. It's resilient stuff and develops so many different flavours as it gently warms up in the glass and opens out.

I've been lucky enough to break bread with a number of first-class sparkling winemakers, not only in champagne but around the world, and I've had some fine, shirt-popping meals with them. And, as you might expect, each and every one has told me how well their fizz goes with food. You might think they would, wouldn't they?

Well, you can always see for yourself. And in an effort to encourage you to do so, I herewith give you my top ten matches.

CAVA AND TAPAS
It's what they do in Barcelona and with good reason.

PROSECCO AND SUSHI
The slight sweetness of the former contrasts beautifully with the soy sauce saltiness of the latter.

BRUT NON-VINTAGE CHAMPAGNE WITH
SMOKED SALMON AND/OR OYSTERS
C'mon, they're an obvious match!

ROSÉ CHAMPAGNE WITH ROAST PORK OR VEAL
Well, there's lots of Pinot Noir in the fizz so don't be surprised how well it works.

OLD CHAMPAGNE (VINTAGE OR NON) WITH
MUSHROOM OR TRUFFLE RISOTTO
The fizz will have mushroom and truffle notes of its own, leading to a perfect pairing.

SWEET CHAMPAGNE WITH HARD OR SALTY
CHEESES OR CREAMY, STRAWBERRY DESSERTS
Matches made in heaven.

MOSCATO D'ASTI WITH FRUIT TARTS
You'll wonder why you've never paired them before.

SWEET LAMBRUSCO WITH GRILLED PEACHES
Yum!

SPARKLING AUSTRALIAN SYRAH WITH THE
BEEFIEST THING ON THE BARBIE
As any Aussie will tell you, it just works.

CANADIAN SPARKLING ICEWINE WITH... NOTHING
Have it on its own at the end of the meal as the perfect palate-cleanser.

CLOUDY BAY PELORUS NV

MARLBOROUGH, NEW ZEALAND

Everyone has heard of Cloudy Bay in New Zealand and mighty fine its wines are, too. The standard Cloudy Bay Sauvignon Blanc and Pinot Noir are excellent fare and the wild ferment, oak-aged Te Koko Sauvignon Blanc is really very special indeed and well worth seeking out if you've not tried it.

Cloudy Bay occasionally comes in for a bit of a bashing, which I've always thought unfair. Maybe because it's owned by the vast LVMH conglomerate and maybe because its wines aren't cheap, folk feel able to take a pop at it. It's a shame, though, for as I say, the wines are first rate, and it was Cloudy Bay that truly put New Zealand on the wine map.

Cloudy Bay might not have been the first actually to plant Sauvignon Blanc in New Zealand; that honour goes to the pioneering Spence brothers of Matua Valley Wines, who produced the first Kiwi Sauvignon Blanc at their vineyard near Auckland in 1974. But Cloudy Bay was the first to take the variety seriously, and to market it with any great success.

David Hohnen of Cape Mentelle, in Australia's Margaret River, had tasted some of the Spence brothers' wines and was so impressed that he was prompted to found Cloudy Bay in Marlborough, at the top of New Zealand's South Island, in 1985. LVMH bought the estate (along with Cape Mentelle) in 1990, and it remains the best known of all Kiwi wines.

Pelorus is Cloudy Bay's fizz and I love it. It is named after Pelorus Jack, a celebrated dolphin that used to guide ships through the Cook Strait in the late 1800s/early 1900s; the animal is commemorated on the neck label by a stylized golden dolphin.

Made using the traditional method, Pelorus is a blend of Chardonnay and Pinot Noir that spends two years on the lees. It is crisp, clean and refreshing, with hints of apple, citrus and just a touch of toasted brioche.

I reckon it works best as an apéritif rather than with food, although it does partner simple fish dishes and sushi darn well. Either way, it's lovely stuff, surprisingly complex and with a pleasingly long finish.

WWW.CLOUDYBAY.CO.NZ

PERRIER-JOUËT BELLE EPOQUE BLANC DE BLANCS 2004

CHAMPAGNE, FRANCE

I've always had a soft spot for the wines of Perrier-Jouët. Thanks to the generosity of some extremely well-chosen, wine-loving godparents, my wife Marina and I were able to toast the birth of both our sons in 1990 Perrier-Jouët Belle Epoque.

It's a fabulous wine and if there's a prettier champagne bottle than P-J's Belle Epoque with its hand-painted, art nouveau-style anemones curling round the glass, please let me know.

Perrier-Jouët was founded in 1811, and is the stablemate of G.H. Mumm (see page 108) as part of the Pernod Ricard portfolio. Hervé Deschamps is P-J's legendary head winemaker, only the seventh ever to hold that post, remarkably enough. And Monsieur Deschamps makes famously fine wines. The Grand Brut NV and Rosé Blason NV are both all too often overlooked by fans of Belle Epoque, which is a shame, because they're excellent quality and great value too.

Perrier-Jouët is launching, as I write, a brand-new *cuvée* to add to these two: the Perrier-Jouët Blanc de Blancs Brut NV. I've had a sneak preview and it's a belter: 100 per cent Chardonnay and truly exhilarating, fresh and vivacious. There's no doubt that it will soon attract a devoted following.

But will it ever eclipse the fabled Belle Epoque wines? There are three in the range: the vintage Belle Epoque, the vintage Belle Epoque Rosé and the vintage Belle Epoque Blanc de Blancs. For me, it's the last one that is the most eye-catching and exciting. I've remembered each and every time I've tried it. The current vintage is the 2004 and it's the rarest wine in the Perrier-Jouët range. They hardly make any of it at all.

What they do make is produced from two tiny parcels of *grand cru* Chardonnay in the village of Cramant in the heart of the Côte de Blancs. It's instantly appealing, with racy citrus notes, luscious white stone fruit and tantalizing glimpses of vanilla and brioche. Its rarity is reflected in the price and, crikey, it's expensive, but crikey, it's good.

Go find a well-heeled, wine-loving godparent for your nipper and enjoy!

WWW.PERRIER-JOUET.COM

PIPER-HEIDSIECK CUVÉE RARE 2002

CHAMPAGNE, FRANCE

OK, here's your starter for ten. Who has won Sparkling Winemaker of the Year at the International Wine Challenge an unprecedented number of times in the following years, including an astonishing seven in succession: 2004, 2007, 2008, 2009, 2010, 2011, 2012, 2013? Benoît Gouez, the chef de cave at Moët & Chandon, the world's best-selling champagne? Richard Geoffroy, his Moët counterpart at the world's best-known *prestige cuvée* champagne, Dom Pérignon itself? Or how about Pieter 'Bubbles' Ferreira, the genius behind Graham Beck's fabulous fizzes in South Africa?

Well, nope, none of the above. Step forward, please, Régis Camus, the genial and canny mastermind at Piper-Heidsieck, the champagne house that's in the same ownership as Charles Heidsieck (though not Heidsieck Monopole), but which is run completely separately. Founded in 1785, Piper-Heidsieck might be Champagne's third-largest export brand and Monsieur Camus might be covered in plaudits, but I don't reckon the brand gets the recognition it deserves from critics, punters or even wine merchants.

Which is daft, really, because the Piper-Heidsieck Brut NV is a real treat and very well priced and the brut vintage is ditto. It's the *prestige cuvée*, though, the so-called Rare, that really knocks one's socks off.

It's a crazy price but this multi-award-winning, 70 per cent Chardonnay (with fruit drawn only from the Montagne de Reims), 30 per cent Pinot Noir is a remarkable wine. Aged for seven years, it's rich, generous and mouth-filling, full of honeyed brioche and toast. It's also a marvellous food wine, delicious with foie gras, oysters (of course) and a plate of creamy truffle pasta.

The bottle itself is also rather striking, and when you've drained it and feel silly and squiffy you can always peel off its golden wraparound thingy and wear it as a tiara. Don't scoff; it's irresistible and when in their cups it's just what folk do.

WWW.PIPER-HEIDSIECK.COM

PIZZATO ESPUMANTE BRUT ROSÉ 2013

VALE DOS VINHEDOS, BRAZIL

This charming pink fizz comes from the Vale dos Vinhedos in southern Brazil, just down the road from where Miolo makes its Brut Millésime (see page 102). But where Miolo's operation is a vast one, entered via a Hollywood studio-like archway and boasting a shop, visitor centre, barrel hall, bottling line, tasting room, observation tower, gardens, children's play and picnic area and enormous wine spa hotel bang opposite, Pizzato is a much more modest affair, set deep in an atmospheric 'lost' valley at the end of a long pot-holed track near the village of Santa Lucia.

It's a boutique winery for sure, housed in a building bought from a bulk-wine producer who had long abandoned it. Antonio Pizzato arrived here from Breganze, Italy, in 1882, and immediately set about planting grapes. Up until that point, according to Flavio Pizzato – Antonio's great-great-grandson – there was nothing here except forests, stones and monkeys.

It wasn't until 1999, though, that the family started to make wine commercially. Hitherto they had sold grapes to a local cooperative and made only modest amounts for home consumption. Today, Flavio is the one tending the grapes and making the wines, and jolly good they are, too.

He makes still reds and whites here on the family's 26-hectare vineyard and sparklers, too, of which this is my firm favourite. Made in the traditional method from hand-picked fruit (85 per cent Pinot Noir and 15 per cent Chardonnay), it spends nine months on the lees before being disgorged. With wild strawberries, sour and ripe cherries and even – as Flavio points out – a whisper of gingerbread on the palate, it's delectably soft, smooth and extremely drinkable.

WWW.PIZZATO.NET

'CHAMPAGNE SHOULD BE COLD, DRY AND HOPEFULLY, FREE.'

CHRISTIAN POL ROGER

POL ROGER VINTAGE 2008

CHAMPAGNE, FRANCE

I'll fess up from the start and declare proudly that Pol Roger is my favourite champagne. Well, if you've stuck with this book thus far you'll know it's actually my equal favourite with Bollinger. I love them both and can't choose between them.

I probably drink slightly more Pol than Bol, largely because Pol Roger is pretty much the house pour at the *Spectator*, at which magazine I'm lucky enough to be the drinks editor. Not that we drink it all the time – just most of the time. There are certainly more bottles of Pol Roger in the office fridge than there are of milk and it's a fact that no party of note or celebration at the *Spectator* passes by without several bottles of Pol being broached and hugely enjoyed.

Sadly, the *Spectator*'s (and my) budget can only stretch to the non-vintage Pol Roger, familiar to many wine lovers thanks to its distinctive white foil neck. Famously, Pol was Sir Winston Churchill's favourite champagne. He even went so far as to name his racehorse Pol Roger. It's said that the great man got through more than 500 cases of Pol Roger in the last ten years of his life, leading his daughter, Lady Soames, to remark, 'I saw him many times the better for it, but never the worse.'

Pol Vintage is something else altogether and I was lucky enough to be invited to sample the 2008 Brut Vintage at Pol Roger HQ in Avenue de Champagne, Épernay (the world's most drinkable address, according to Churchill), just before it was launched. I was quite stunned by its quality.

A typical Pol blend of 60 per cent Pinot Noir and 40 per cent Chardonnay drawn from 20 *grands* and *premiers crus* vineyards, the wine matured for eight years in Pol Roger's chalk cellars – the deepest in the region, the maze of corridors stretching for some 7km (4 miles) – before being released.

The resulting wine is wonderfully toasty and rich, with whispers of honey, nuts, mushrooms, truffles and even a touch of spice. And as I wrote in the *Spectator*, it's without doubt the finest Pol Roger I've ever tasted, and exactly what fine vintage champagne is all about.

WWW.POLROGER.COM

FRATELLI PONTE FIORE DI LOTO MOSCATO D'ASTI 2015

PIEDMONT, ITALY

I don't care what you say, but no book on fizz such as this could possibly omit Asti, formerly known as Asti Spumante. I know it's seen as irredeemably passé and too redolent of the cheesy seventies by knowing sophisticates, but at its best – as here – it can just be so charming and such fun.

In fact, to be strictly accurate, this example is a Moscato d'Asti, which is ever so slightly different from Asti Spumante in that it's marginally less fizzy and marginally lighter in alcohol. Other than that, both wines are the same: fizzy; originating from near Asti in Piedmont; and made from 100 per cent Moscato Bianco (aka Muscat Blanc à Petits Grains).

Family-owned Fratelli Ponte has been making wine for 50 years and is particularly known for its red Barbera d'Asti and Barolo and for its white Arneis. This Moscato d'Asti is a frothy and joyful diversion. It's tank-fermented and vibrantly fresh, floral and aromatic. It smells just so enticing and so, well, grapily delicious.

It's *frizzante* – that's to say, semi-sparkling or *pétillant* – rather than full-on fizzy and once the fermenting grape juice reaches 5.5%vol, the process is stopped, leaving it low in alcohol and high in natural sugar.

Moscato d'Asti has always been the wine that the winemakers drink themselves during lunch, as it's so fresh, so sweet and so light in alcohol. On summer holidays my dear old dad got into just such a habit, too, albeit by bringing forward uncorking time to 11A.M. rather than the winemakers' more usual 12.30P.M. Indeed, on one occasion, enlivened by a couple of glasses, he was moved to pen the following lines:

My God, he's an impudent fella!
That girl that he showed round the cellar
Lost her *status quo ante*
Between the Chianti
And the magnums of Valpolicella…

Which reminds me of Asti Spumante,
A wine that I'm more *pro* than *anti* –
The only thing is
That this fizz aphrodis-
-iac leads to *delicto flagrante*…

Go on, have some. you'll love it!
WWW.FRATELLIPONTEVINI.IT

REICHSRAT VON BUHL
RIESLING BRUT SEKT 2014

PFALZ, GERMANY

Corral any group of wine writers, wine merchants or sommeliers together (I wonder what the collective noun for such a body would be: a glug? A slosh?) and despite the fact that they will have spent the previous few hours extolling the virtues to their readers or customers of Meursault, Chablis, Sancerre, Pouilly-Fumé, white Rhône, California Chardonnay or Hunter Valley Semillon, I bet that all they'll want to drink is Riesling (unless of course they opt to sneak in a swift bone-dry manzanilla sherry).

It reminds me of Karl Barth's celebrated comment, that when the angels sing to God, they sing Bach, but that when they sing to themselves, they sing Mozart. Not that for a minute would I equate the bunch of lushes I'm talking about with angels. But Riesling (and BTW, it's *reez-ling*, not *rise-ling*) is a true delight. It thrives in Alsace and in such blessed spots as Australia's Barossa and Clare valleys, New Zealand's Marlborough and Elgin in South Africa. Germany, though, is its spiritual home. It can be dry, off-dry or rampantly, richly, tongue-coatingly sweet. It never sees oak and so is never less than crisp, clean and utterly pure. Very occasionally, as a bit of a sideline, it can be deliciously, enticingly effervescent.

I think it's fair to say that Reichsrat von Buhl, an estate founded in 1849, went into a bit of a dip not so long ago. Today, though, it's firing on all cylinders, not least thanks to the arrival in 2013 of Mathieu Kauffmann, the former chef de cave at mighty Bollinger, no less. Here he has crafted a gorgeous, traditional method, 100-per-cent Riesling sparkler. It's utterly delicious: crisp, concentrated and apple-fresh with underlying citrus notes and a whistle-clean finish.

I'm told that Mathieu Kauffmann has even finer fizzes slumbering in the von Buhl cellars, biding their time. All I have to say is this fizz is more than good enough to be going on with until they're ready.

WWW.VON-BUHL.DE

RIDGEVIEW FITZROVIA ROSÉ BRUT 2014

EAST SUSSEX, ENGLAND

Ridgeview, near Ditchling, East Sussex, is almost exactly 16km (10 miles) away from my house in Brighton – a mere 23-minute drive. It's my local winery and I couldn't be prouder to have it on my doorstep. In fairness, according to the *AA Route Planner*, it's exactly the same distance away from me as Breaky Bottom (see page 40), but since that's in the middle of nowhere and you have to allow an extra 20 minutes just for the potholes and the sheep, it takes appreciably longer to get to. But how lucky am I to have two such fine wineries so close? And there are many more only slightly further afield, with around 70 vineyards (not all stretch to their own winery) in East and West Sussex alone.

Ridgeview is seriously fine. Founded in 1995 by the late, great and extremely genial Mike Roberts, the estate is now in the hands of his widow, Chris, daughter Tamara, son Simon and Simon's Aussie wife, Mardi. They make a formidable team, and Ridgeview simply goes from strength to strength.

The first Ridgeview wines were launched in 2000, since when they've picked up an absurd amount of garlands, awards and medals. In 2006, the 2004 Ridgeview Blanc de Blancs was served at the Queen's eightieth birthday banquet. HM enjoyed it so much that she served the 2002 Ridgeview Rosé to Barack Obama during his state visit in 2011. The following year, Ridgeview Bloomsbury was declared the official fizz of the Queen's Diamond Jubilee and in 2016 it was declared ditto of 10 Downing Street. Forgive me if I seem to be belabouring the point, but a few years ago it would have been unthinkable for the great and the good to serve anything other than fine vintage champagne. Thanks to the likes of Ridgeview, though, English sparkling wine has come such a long way.

I have tried every one of Ridgeview's many cuvées and I love them all. My favourite, though, is the 2014 Ridgeview Fitzrovia Rosé: a fabulous salmon-pink blend of Chardonnay (50 per cent), Pinot Noir (33 per cent) and Pinot Meunier (17 per cent). It's spot-on – the perfect summer apéritif and one that my neighbours happily imbibe whenever I crack some open.

WWW.RIDGEVIEW.CO.UK

WHAT BEST TO CALL ENGLISH FIZZ

France has champagne and crémant. Spain has Cava; South Africa has Méthode Cap Classique; Canada has Méthode Classique and Italy has Franciacorta. All these are terms for sparkling wines made in the so-called traditional method. Italy also has non-traditional method Prosecco, too, of course.

What do we in the UK have? English sparkling wine. It hardly trips off the tongue, does it? Producers and consumers have long agonized over what simple term to give our native fizzes, but nobody can agree. Some wonder, why bother.

Christian Seely of Coates & Seely in Hampshire wants to use the term Britagne, which nobody seems to know how to pronounce. Mark Driver of Rathfinny Wine Estate in East Sussex (who at the time of writing hasn't even produced any fizz) wants to patent the name Sussex. But what about makers of fine English fizz elsewhere?

In an effort to solve this vinous puzzle, we ran a competition in the *Spectator* recently, asking readers to come up with a less-cumbersome term than 'English sparkling wine' to describe our wonderful native vino. My fellow judge was Wendy Outhwaite QC, barrister-turned-winemaker at Ambriel, in West Sussex.

As I wrote at the time, we had some fine entries – clever, apposite, droll and even occasionally rather convoluted – as well as the inevitable late-at-night-after-a-bottle-or-so ones. Yes, yes, I'm talking about you at the back, Fizzy McFizz Face.

One reader reckoned we should stick with English sparkling wine ('No sense in confusing the customer') while another reckoned that since we're leaving the EU we should stick one in the eye of the French and call our fizz champagne since we might no longer be bound by EU-protected drink names. Several readers suggested such Frenchified terms as Cru Anglais, Cuvée Anglaise, Éblouissant, Anglais Bolle and Crémant Bretagne, which seems somehow to miss the point, and many suggested Albion or its variants, which doesn't.

Some came over all Middle English with Saxone and Spearclen (sparkling); some came over all Latin with Britannia Prima and Vinbulla – which sounded a bit like a nasty skin condition but was in fact cleverly derived from *vinum* for wine and *bulla* for bubble – and Maxima, 'From *Maxima Caesariensis*, denoting the South East of England, to satisfy neatly the competing counties with an all-encompassing name.' But what about West Country fizz?

Some suggested terms that harked back to our past, such as Iceni, and others that harked back to historical figures, such as Boudicca, Asquith, Kitchener and Merret (after Christopher Merret, the English scientist who delivered a paper on sparkling wines to the Royal Society in 1662, but whose name is already in use by the producer Ridgeview in Sussex). Someone suggested Grenadier, and a couple of folk (I thought there'd be more) suggested Farage.

There were witty but rather too ephemeral suggestions, such as Britpop (one of my favourites), Splosh, Shampain, Merrie, Anglosia, Blighty Bubbles, Cork Blimey. And there were, of course, one or two hilarious ones far too rude to print.

After much agonizing, however, Wendy and I finally decided that the best term for English sparkling wine was simply Britannia. Maybe a bit obvious, but it's dramatic, familiar, easy to pronounce and remember and, in its way, rather noble. We declared this the winner.

A week or so later, though, I changed my mind. Why don't we just call our wine crémant? Yes, yes, I know: it's a French term. But it's short, pithy, to the point and already has a strict, officially sanctioned meaning. Producers in France and Luxembourg are happy with it and consumers know exactly what it means.

Waiter! A large glass of chilled English crémant, please!

'I COULD NOT
CONJURE UP ONE
MELANCHOLY FANCY
UPON A MUTTON
CHOP AND A GLASS
OF CHAMPAGNE.'

JEROME K. JEROME, *IDLE THOUGHTS
OF AN IDLE FELLOW*

LOUIS ROEDERER
BRUT PREMIER NV

CHAMPAGNE, FRANCE

Louis Roederer is one of the few remaining independent, family-run champagne houses (along with the likes of Bollinger, Taittinger and Pol Roger), and while it's rightly proud of its entire range, it's Cristal, that most swanky of champagnes, for which the house is best known. As Michel Janneau, Roederer's executive vice-president, once told me, 'If champagne is special, then Cristal is special-special.'

Long beloved by well-heeled nightclubbers, Cristal famously fell out of favour with such folk after some ill judged comments from Frédéric Rouzaud, Louis Roederer's MD and representative of the family's seventh generation (see page 130). The wine remains exceptional quality, though, and it's fair to say that there was a collective sigh of relief from certain wine lovers once the rappers and footballers had left the scene.

It was, however, the original celebrity champagne, created especially for a Russian tsar. Alexander II had asked that a unique champagne be produced for his own personal use. Some say that the bottle was made of clear crystal so that the tsar could see whether the liquid had been adulterated with poison; others that it was simply to show off the golden hue of the wine more elegantly. It's also said that the bottle was produced without an indentation (punt) in the bottom in order to prove to the suspicious tsar that he wasn't being given short measure, or maybe it was to strengthen the bottle, or even to prevent a small bomb being put under it. Who knows? The fact is that Cristal has a mythology all its own.

Its price puts it beyond most of us hoi polloi, though, and that's why I suggest aiming for the Louis Roederer Brut Premier NV. It's beautifully made, a blend of 40 per cent Chardonnay, 40 per cent Pinot Noir and 20 per cent Pinot Meunier, with a touch of oak ageing. In fact, I would say that it's sheer class in a glass, with famously fine bubbles, a rich, creamy texture and a long finish.

If you want an immaculately made champagne that's not unfairly priced and yet still boasts a bit of the Cristal stardust, then this one is for you.

WWW.LOUIS-ROEDERER.COM

ROEDERER QUARTET
ANDERSON VALLEY BRUT ROSÉ NV

CALIFORNIA, USA

Roederer Estate is the Californian outpost of family-owned champagne house Louis Roederer, and was founded in 1982. The timber, rustic-looking winery and tasting room lie just north of Philo, in cool-climate Anderson Valley. Anderson is one of the 12 officially designated American Viticultural Areas (AVAs) of Mendocino County, the administrative centre of which is Ukiah (the name will be familiar, I'm sure, to fans of the Doobie Brothers). It's ruggedly beautiful and unspoiled here, with rolling, wooded hills and valleys filled with mist and fog that steal in from the nearby Pacific, and I'm told that barely 3 per cent of the region is either inhabited or farmed.

Mendocino County was much favoured by the Haight-Ashbury, 'Summer of Love' generation and was a magnet for flower-power folk escaping San Francisco in search of rural peace. I spent a couple of days there a few years back, pottering about, tasting the wines and hanging out, and was not in the least surprised to learn that Mendocino's biggest cash crop has long been marijuana.

Grapes, though, is its second biggest, and it was these rather than the promise of fine California grass that brought the Roederer-owning Rouzaud family out here in the eighties. They bought four estates in Boonville, Philo and Navarro (hence the name Quartet) and set about making first-rate California fizz with a French twist.

Their super, salmon-pink rosé is a blend of 56 per cent Pinot Noir and 44 per cent Chardonnay, entirely estate-grown. Oak-aged reserve wines contribute up to about 20 per cent of the blend and the resulting wine is just so tasty, full of really quite delicate wild strawberry and redcurrant fruit backed by a long, smooth, rounded finish.

WWW.ROEDERERESTATE.COM

RUCA MALEN SPARKLING BRUT TRADITIONAL METHOD NV

MENDOZA, ARGENTINA

The Uco Valley in Argentina's Mendoza is one of the most spectacular of all wine regions, with stunning – both architecturally and technologically – state-of-the-art wineries, vineyards almost as far as the eye can see, and the staggering, swaggering snow-capped Andes in the distance. The weather, too, is heavenly. If they get any fewer than 330 straight days of sunshine here, they feel short-changed.

This is Malbec country, of course. Vineyards are planted at high altitude, where it's sunny but cool and the quality of fruit is remarkable: fully ripened grapes with thick skins, which is great for colour, structure and silky tannins. When I was last there I drank nothing but big, butch, violet-scented Malbecs for an entire week. And I ate nothing but saddle-sized slabs of beef without so much as a hint of anything green to keep malnutrition at bay. I went a bit stir-crazy.

On my final day I found myself craving some leaves of lettuce or morsels of sushi and something light, refreshing and preferably sparkling to drink. And so it was that I met this little charmer: a traditional method sparkler from Bodega Ruca Malen (the name, apparently, means 'The house of the young girl', after a local legend of the old tribes that inhabited the area).

I already knew of Ruca Malen's fabulous Malbecs – indeed, I'd sunk a few that very week – but their fizz was new to me and I was entranced. A hand-harvested, bottle-fermented blend of 75 per cent Pinot Noir and 25 per cent Chardonnay, it's fresh, lively and creamy, with toasted nuts and brioche lightened by crisp, ripe, citrus notes. It was the perfect antidote to a week's worth of hearty Malbecs and I loved it. I still do.

WWW.BODEGARUCAMALEN.COM

RUINART BLANC DE BLANCS BRUT NV

CHAMPAGNE, FRANCE

Ask any wine merchant or sommelier to name his or her favourite champagnes and I can guarantee that Ruinart would be in everyone's top three, or in their top five at the very least. It's a producer of spectacular champagnes and one which, for some reason, just doesn't get the credit it deserves outside the trade.

Ruinart was founded in 1729 by Nicolas Ruinart, nephew of Dom Ruinart, after whom the house's *prestige cuvée* is named and who lies buried a few feet away from his friend, fellow winemaker and Benedictine monk, Dom Pérignon, in the ruined Abbey of Saint Peter of Hautvillers set high above the Marne Valley.

It's the trick question beloved of wine buffs: which is the oldest producer in champagne? Well, Ruinart is the oldest sparkling wine producer in Champagne but Gosset (see page 73) is the oldest *wine* producer in Champagne, having been founded in 1584, but only to make still wines in those days, of course. Either way, Ruinart, now part of the LVMH empire, is a name to conjure with. Its most popular wine of all is this peachy non-vintage Blanc de Blancs. Made from 100-per-cent Chardonnay drawn from the finest sites in the Côte des Blancs and Montagne de Reims, it's wonderfully clean, aromatic, fresh and focused, with buckets of zesty citrus flavours, creamy peaches and a fleeting hint of honeysuckle.

I simply love it and love its distinctive, rounded bottle shape, too (the half-bottles are even prettier), inspired by the original champagne bottles of the eighteenth century. It's a great champagne and shouldn't just be enjoyed by those in the know.

WWW.RUINART.COM

DOMAINE STE MICHELLE BRUT NV

WASHINGTON STATE, USA

They make wine in every state in America these days, or so
I'm told. The mind boggles. Of course, the finest American
wines, such as those from the Napa Valley, say, Sonoma County
or Mendocino, California, are famously among the best in
the world. The worst American wines, though, are famously
unspeakable and rarely produced from classic *Vitis vinifera*
grapes. That's if they're made from grapes at all. The four
wineries in Alaska, for example, make wine from other
fruits entirely.

I remember having some extremely grim, locally made,
'Cha-blee' in Bubba's Diner in Hannibal, Missouri, once many
years ago. Hannibal, the boyhood home of Mark Twain, is not
known for the quality of its cuisine and I'm not sure which
was worse: the wine or the deep-fried catfish and onion rings
(which were sold by the foot). The sign outside the door
exhorted Bubba's customers to 'Walk in, Waddle Out', which
might give you some idea o f the establishment's flavour.

Washington State is America's third-largest wine-producing state
after California and New York, and the second-largest when it
comes to the production of premium wine (with Oregon and
Virginia following). The wines here, thankfully, are excellent.

Vines were first planted in 1825 by the Hudson's Bay Company.
In 1938 there were 42 wineries in the state; today there are over
900, with 40 per cent of vineyards planted in the last ten years.
They tell me that a new winery opens every 15 days and that
winemaking in Washington has become a $4.4bn plus industry.

Château Ste Michelle was one of the pioneers, planting its
first *Vitis vinifera* vines in 1967 under the aegis of legendary
winemaker André Tchelistcheff. Today, it has two state-of-the-
art wineries and produces exceptional still and sparkling wines.

This entry-level traditional method fizz from northerly
vineyards in the cool-climate Columbia Valley is fresh, lively
and immediately appealing. It's not what you might call
complex but, blended from 60 per cent Chardonnay and 20 per
cent each of Pinot Noir and Pinot Gris, it's full of light citrus
and green-apple flavours set off by delicious frothy and creamy
mousse. It makes the perfect summer apéritif.

WWW.MICHELLESPARKLING.COM

IL GRILLO DI SANTA TRESA
VINO SPUMANTE BIOLOGICO
BRUT NV

SICILY, ITALY

First, a confession and not one I'm proud to make: I've never been to Sicily. I know, I know, but there you are, I've said it now. I'd hate you to think that I was a complete Philistine, however, for *The Leopard* is one of my favourite books and I've seen the film too (many times). I've often been to Venice (attentive readers will know that I even got engaged there, thanks to a Bellini fuelled rush of blood to the head in Harry's Bar) and am familiar with Rome, Florence, Bologna, Siena, Milan, Naples, the Amalfi coast, Puglia, Le Marche and so on. Somehow, though, Sicily has slipped through the net. It's my loss, as everyone keeps saying, and it's not for want of trying. It has just never worked out.

One reason I particularly want to go is to visit Feudo di Santa Tresa, in the deep south of the island. It is an estate that has been home to winemaking since 1697 and which, since 2002, has been in the hands of Stefano Girelli, his sister Marina Girelli, and Massimo Maggio: a pioneering trio producing fabulous, well-priced certified organic wines from Sicily's native varieties.

A year or so ago we had a tasting of the estate's entire range at the *Spectator* offices, and everyone present was bowled over by the wines' quality and by their sense of place. They were truly unique. Although Santa Tresa uses state-of-the-art equipment and techniques, it's intent on also using traditional, local grape varieties. So it is, for example, that the Cabernet Sauvignon the winemaking team inherited is being phased out in favour of the local Perricone, a grape better suited to the local terroir.

They grow Nero d'Avola here, Fiano, Frappato and Grillo; from the latter they make this utterly charming organic, tank method sparkler. It's light, dry, lemony fresh with a deliciously creamy mousse and zesty acidity. I can only imagine (never having been there) what a perfect drink it would be for a hot Sicilian summer evening on the terrace.

If you like Prosecco you'll love it. You might even prefer it.

WWW.SANTATRESA.COM

SCHRAMSBERG
BLANC DE BLANCS BRUT 2013

CALIFORNIA, USA

I visited Schramsberg Vineyards years ago on my first trip to the Napa Valley and I've never forgotten the effect my initial sip of Schramsberg fizz had on me. The wines had been bigged up to me mightily by my hosts, and the more they banged on about how fine they were, the more I thought them bragging but deluded fools. In my blinkered naivety, I thought that no sparkling wine could possibly compare with the wines of Champagne, especially not a sparkling wine from California or anywhere else in the so-called New World.

Within a trice I realized what a snobbish, brainwashed buffoon I was. The wine was stunning and I understood immediately why Schramsberg was a wine impossible to ignore. My hosts were charming and gracious in the face of my pink-faced embarrassment. They were delighted, too, that I had discovered what they had long known: that Schramsberg, the first producer of top-quality fizz in California – in the entire country in fact – remained its finest, a true world-beater. Not for nothing has it been served at official state functions by every American presidential administration since President Nixon's famous 'Toast to Peace' with Chinese Premier Zhou Enlai in 1972.

Schramsberg Vineyards, on Diamond Mountain, near Calistoga, was founded in 1862 by Jacob Schram, an immigrant from Pfeddersheim in Germany. He made still, not sparkling, wines here, but the estate fell into decline after his death and was eventually abandoned. In 1965 it was bought by Jack and Jamie Davies, who were intent on making fine sparkling wine in California, which they succeeded in doing with knobs on. Today the winery is in the hands of Jack and Jamie's son, Hugh.

There are a number of fizzes in the Schramsberg range, but it's this Blanc de Blancs that I find the most delectable. Made from 100 per cent Chardonnay harvested from the best vineyard sites in the Napa Valley, Sonoma County, Mendocino and Marin County, part of the blend is fermented in oak barrels.

It is ripe, crisp and fresh, with perfectly rounded fruit in the mouth and a long, toasty finish. If you've never had a Schramsberg sparkler, you're in for a treat.

WWW.SCHRAMSBERG.COM

SIMONNET-FEBVRE
CRÉMANT DE BOURGOGNE
BRUT P100 BLANC DE NOIR NV

BURGUNDY, FRANCE

Although this is the only traditional method sparkling wine made in Chablis, it's much more than just a charming curiosity: it's completely delicious. Classified as a Crémant de Bourgogne (the term crémant referring to those French sparkling wines made using the traditional method of production but outside the region of Champagne itself), it's made by Jean-Philippe Archambaud, head winemaker and managing director of Simonnet-Febvre.

Established in 1840 and now part of the Louis Latour empire, Simonnet-Febvre is best known for its top-quality *grand* and *premier cru* Chablis, but it also makes regional wines such as Côte d'Auxerre and Irancy, and – of particular interest to us – white and rosé sparkling wines of real style. Before arriving at Simonnet-Febvre in 2004, Jean-Philippe spent many years working for Rhône legend Michel Chapoutier, both in France and at his Australian outpost, and he is as neat and natty a winemaker as he is a neat and natty dresser (J-P is the only man I have ever seen pull off the brown corduroy suit, tie and wellies look in a vineyard) and certainly knows his stuff.

I can't praise his Brut P100 Blanc de Noir enough. Made from 100 per cent Pinot Noir, it's dry but rich, creamy, toasty and biscuity, too, touched with a hint of citrus. We have often offered this wine to readers of the *Spectator* via our Wine Club and it sells out every time. And little wonder, for it's absurdly tasty and a copper-bottomed bargain.

I've had champagnes three times the price that I liked three times less.

WWW.SIMONNET-FEBVRE.COM

SO JENNIE PARIS ALCOHOL-FREE SPARKLING ROSÉ NV

FRANCE/BELGIUM

So there I was in the Qatar Airways Premium Lounge in Heathrow airport, hobnobbing with my fellow business and first-class passengers. Oh don't be silly; I wasn't paying for it. I was on press trip, otherwise known as scrounging a freebie.

Be that as it may, I was acutely aware of being way beyond my pay grade and I was determined to make the most of it. The food was of an astonishingly high quality, and if I tell you that the fizzes on offer included the likes of Krug Grande Cuvée, Laurent-Perrier Grand Siècle, Pol Roger Vintage, Veuve Clicquot's La Grande Dame and Bollinger's La Grande Année, you will get some idea of how far beyond my pay grade I was.

And there, rubbing shoulders with such haughty champagnes, was this: So Jennie Paris. I'd never heard of it and didn't know what it was. Turns out it's a sugar-free, alcohol-free sparkler created in France and bottled in Belgium.

A *what??*

Now, I don't 'do' non-alcoholic drinks. I'm extremely suspicious of such things. As far as I'm concerned, it's alcohol or Badoit (which, actually, I love), with nothing in between. I particularly look down upon alcohol-free drinks masquerading as alcoholic ones. It's like those ghastly vegan sausages made out of lentil dust and some vile meat-free paste but made to look like, well, good old-fashioned sausages. And have you ever had a decent alcohol-free lager? They all taste of soap powder.

Anyway, entirely out of academic interest and prepared to scoff and sneer mightily, I tried the So Jennie. And blow me, it was a cracker! Pale pink in colour, it was light, effervescent and wonderfully refreshing. Not for a second did I feel short-changed by the lack of alcohol.

I'm not entirely sure how it's made, other than it's produced from grape must extracts and has no added sugars, no alcohol, no sulphites, no additives, no preservatives and hardly any calories. The bottle looks extremely proper and the fizz in the glass looks like the finest champagne. It's absolutely perfect for anyone who doesn't want to – or can't – drink alcohol.

WWW.SOJENNIE.PARIS

THE SOCIETY'S CHAMPAGNE BRUT NV

CHAMPAGNE, FRANCE

If I was told, for whatever bizarre reason, that I was to be allowed only to buy wine from one retailer for the rest of my life, I know exactly where I would head: to The Wine Society (WS), of course, the world's oldest cooperative wine club, founded in 1874.

At the time of writing, the WS is both the current International Wine Challenge Merchant of the Year and the Online Retailer of the Year, and its many and varied wines are incredibly keenly priced, thanks to the fact that the society is owned by its members and exists purely for their benefit.

Joining is simple: just buy one (£40/US$52) share and you – or whoever you're treating   become a member for life. Oh, and the WS will give you credit towards your first order. There are over 1,500 wines to choose from on their list, with over 300 wines priced at £7.95 (US$10) or less, and the quality of the own-label Society and Exhibition wines, in particular, is legendary. There are also regular tastings for members across the UK, and I cannot think of a single reason why somebody wouldn't want to join.

The society's own-label champagne is a cracker and one that I've often enjoyed. A blend of 45 per cent Chardonnay, 28 per cent Pinot Noir and 27 per cent Pinot Meunier, it's produced expressly for the WS by Alfred Gratien, one of the more traditional champagne producers and with whom the WS has been in cahoots since 1906.

Alfred Gratien still ferments its wines in oak, and as a result this is gloriously rich and toasty but with a deliciously fine and refreshing citrus acidity, too. It's impossible not to enjoy.

WWW.THEWINESOCIETY.COM

RÉSERVE DE SOURS
SPARKLING ROSÉ NV

BORDEAUX, FRANCE

Bordeaux is not exactly what you might call the centre of sparkling wine production. But I think one can forgive the Bordelais their shortcomings in this department. After all, they have their hands pretty much full producing some really quite tasty red wines, or so I've heard. And the dry and sweet whites of Bordeaux aren't that bad either, apparently.

No, I never drink fizz in Bordeaux. It just never occurs to me. And I never think to drink Crémant de Bordeaux back home, either. With one glorious exception: the Réserve de Sours Sparkling Rosé. It never fails to lift my spirits.

It comes from the celebrated Château de Sours, a tip-top, 85-hectare estate southwest of Libourne, facing Saint-Émilion, that's dedicated to making the best possible rosé wines. And that's the key: it's a rosé estate that also happens to make a sparkling wine rather than a sparkling wine estate that happens to make a rosé.

All the château's rosé-making expertise goes into making this glorious, bright, salmon-pink blend of Cabernet Sauvignon and Merlot. It's made in the traditional method, spends 16 months on the lees before disgorgement and has style in abundance. It's full of ripe, summery, red berry fruits with touches of cream and baked pastry and has a fine, frothy mousse and a long, dry finish.

It's a first-rate fizz, to be sure: ideal for lazy summer picnics by a river or evenings on the terrace. It's ridiculously cheerful and approachable and as good as many a twice-the-price champagne.

WWW.CHATEAUDESOURS.COM

SPEE'WAH CROOKED MICK CUVÉE CHARDONNAY NV

VICTORIA/NSW, AUSTRALIA

OK, so this is never going to have the good folk of Bollinger, Pol Roger or Ruinart quaking in their boots. And I doubt very much that it would make it onto anybody's list of ten desert-island wines. But if drunk with the right friends, on the right occasion, in the right place, it could easily bring a smile to your lips and put a spring in your step as it did with me. After all, the perfect fizz doesn't always have to be brow-furrowingly complex or cost the earth.

This is a cheap and, to my mind, extremely cheerful fizz from the Murray Darling, Australia's second-largest wine region, which sprawls across northwest Victoria and western New South Wales. It's produced and owned by Qualia Wines which specializes in branded and made-to-order wines, in this case for Bibendum Wine, which sells it exclusively to the on-trade. It's more than likely, therefore, that you'll have seen this on the list at your favourite local eaterie.

The Spee'Wah is a vast, mythical, indefinable area in Australia that's home to wildly improbable tall stories, and the name has been given to a range of modestly priced wines, of which this is the only fizz. Made from 100 per cent Chardonnay fermented in stainless-steel vats and then injected with carbon dioxide, it's undemanding, fresh, citrussy, aromatic and appealing.

It's easy to be snobbish about such wines, but it's extremely drinkable and wonderfully approachable. I first came across it on holiday in Greece, of all places, and as I sat dangling my toes in the sea, picking at some taramasalata and salt-and-pepper squid, glass of Spee'Wah fizz in hand, surrounded by chums, I could not have been happier.

WWW.QWS.COM.AU

TAITTINGER
COMTES DE CHAMPAGNE 2006

CHAMPAGNE, FRANCE

I don't know if you remember that bit in *Casino Royale* (the novel, not the film) where James Bond orders some 1945 Taittinger with his dinner? Bond being Bond knows his wines, of course, but the sommelier manages to persuade him to drink the 1943 Blanc de Blanc [*sic*] Brut from the same house instead.

'That is not a well-known brand,' Bond tells his companion, Vesper Lynd, 'but it is probably the finest champagne in the world.' As soon as he says this, Bond realizes he is being pretentious and explains that it is only because, 'I take such a ridiculous pleasure in what I eat and drink.'

That 1943 fizz was the precursor to the 2006 Taittinger Comtes de Champagne Blanc de Blancs, the company's *prestige cuvée* that was first launched in 1952. And 007 wasn't far off the mark, for although it is not exactly the finest champagne in the world (what is?), it's not far off at all.

Family-owned Taittinger produces famously fine champagnes and the Comtes de Champagne is top of the pile. There have only been thirty vintages of it and this, the 2006, is the most recent. It is made from 100 per cent Chardonnay, from the finest sites, and only the first pressing of the juice is used. A tiny part of the blend is aged in new oak, after which the wine sits deep in Taittinger's chalk cellars for ten years before release.

The result is a wine of staggering complexity and style and, from a marketing perspective, a wine that doesn't shout about itself like some *prestige cuvées* do. Its image is subtle and understated: a wine for those in the know rather than those wanting to show off.

As for what's actually in the bottle, it's dry, of course, but so rich, creamy and profound, full of toast, fresh ripe pears, baked apples and even a touch of toffee. I would say that it's nigh on impossible not to fall in love with.

WWW.TAITTINGER.COM

L'INSTANT
TAITTINGER

CHAMPAGNE TARLANT ROSÉ ZERO BRUT NATURE NV

CHAMPAGNE, FRANCE

It was my old chum David Roberts MW (Master of Wine), of wine merchant Goedhuis & Co, who first tipped me the wink about *la famille* Tarlant's artisanal champagnes, raving about their quality. And he's not even their agent/importer, that honour going to Charles Taylor Fine Wines of London SW1.

David kindly split a bottle of Tarlant Réserve Brut NV with me a while back and I was immediately taken by how fresh, pure and expressive the wine was. It was an utter delight. Even better was the Tarlant Cuvée Louis I had at a later date: a single-vineyard, old-vine, zero-dosage, barrel-fermented, half-and-half blend of Pinot Noir and Chardonnay. An ocean-going belter if ever there was one: so rich, so creamy and so full. I was quite dazzled by it.

The wine I've enjoyed most, though, during my relatively recent love affair with Tarlant, is the Rosé Zero Brut Nature, the current version being a blend of the 2008 and 2009 vintages, aged for six years on the lees.

Getting a brut zero rosé right is tricky, especially one with as much Pinot Noir in it as this one has (some 45 per cent) because with no added sugar, the end result can be a bit tannic. This is most certainly not the case at all here and whatever tannins there are, are more than masked by a plate of accompanying food – and I certainly recommend drinking this alongside some grub. A grilled tuna steak matches it perfectly, as does poached salmon. It also suits fruit tarts beautifully.

The Tarlants have been growing grapes and making wine since 1687, and current winemaker Benoît Tarlant is the twelfth generation of his family to be so employed. What makes their wines so special is their feeling of authenticity, the use of oak for fermentation and maturation, and the consistently low sugar levels; almost all the wines are zero dosage.

This pink fizz is a handmade beauty, so full of red and dark berry fruit with just a hint of honey and a faint but unmistakable zing of white pepper. And it is so fruity you'd never think there was no added sugar.

WWW.TARLANT.COM

DOMAINE JEAN-LOUIS TISSOT
CRÉMANT DU JURA NV

JURA, FRANCE

This just shows what fabulous value you can get in France when you head off the beaten track. And let's be frank: this track is far from beaten, deep in the Jura, in the far eastern reaches of France. It's an anachronistic land that time forgot, tucked between Burgundy and Switzerland. Rather like Norfolk, say, there's no reason to go there unless you're going there, if you see what I mean.

Domaine Jean-Louis Tissot is based in Montigny-lès-Arsures, a tiny commune with just 277 inhabitants in the picture-perfect hills of Franche-Comté, and is run by J-LT's children: Jean-Christophe and Valérie.

The domaine comprises 15 hectares of vineyards where all-but-forgotten local varieties such as Poulsard, Trousseau and Savagnin are grown as well as mainstream varieties such as Pinot Noir and Chardonnay. They make still reds and whites here, as well as Jura's celebrated fino-sherry-like *vin jaune* and this cracking, traditional method fizz or crémant. It's a quirky one for sure, and not one you'll ever see in the aisles of your local supermarket.

But there's something for everyone in the Jura, and savvy sommeliers in the UK are finally cottoning on to the region's delights. In fact, you can work a whole dinner party around the wines of the Jura, and there's no better vino to start with than this sparkling 100-per-cent Chardonnay, which manages to be both biscuity and citrussy and extremely refreshing.

Having tasted it again, I can also say there's no better vino to end with, since it's nigh-on perfect with the hard, creamy and slightly stinky Comté cheese that comes from these parts, or the typical rustic *papet jurassien* tart.

WWW.DOMAINE-JEANLOUIS-TISSOT.COM

MIGUEL TORRES SANTA DIGNA ESTELADO ROSÉ BRUT NV

ITATA VALLEY, CHILE

Even Chileans agree that Chile is quite a ridiculous shape. It's some 4,300km (2,670 miles) long (for the pub quizzers among you, that's roughly the same distance as London to Ouagadougou, capital of Burkina Faso) and an average 177km (110 miles) wide (just 350km [220 miles] at its widest point).

Yet it's a wonderful place for sure and I'm lucky enough to have been several times. There are deserts in the north and ice fields in the south; the Pacific Ocean in the west and Andes Mountains in the east. And as a result of this diverse geography Chile boasts endlessly varied soils, climates and altitudes. Phylloxera – the louse that can devastate grapevines – has never struck, and there are few other vineyard pests. In short, Chile is blessed indeed as a wine-growing country and is home both to big brands as well as independent boutique wineries.

The great Miguel Torres, a titan among Spanish winemakers, was one of the first foreigners to come and make wine here when, in 1979, he bought land and planted vineyards in the Curicó and Central valleys. Today, Miguel Torres Chile (as the family-owned company is known) has some 400 hectares under vine, all of which are certified organic, and it's the largest Fairtrade winery in the country.

And this sparkler of theirs is something rare indeed: the only sparkling wine in the world made from País, an all-but-forgotten grape variety that was first brought to Chile by the Spanish conquistadors in the sixteenth century. The fruit comes from the Itata Valley, a cool-climate region in the heart of Chile, not far from the port city of Concepción, sandwiched between the Maule and Bió-Bió valleys, and the fizz is a pretty pale pink as well as fresh, fruity and vibrant. It's full of ripe redcurrant, pomegranate and zesty citrus and has a long, dry finish.

It makes a great talking-point apéritif and is very well priced.

WWW.MIGUELTORRES.CL

MUSCADELLU
MUSCAT PÉTILLANT NV

CORSICA, FRANCE

Corsica is small but perfectly formed. Roughly half the size of Wales and with a population about the size of Bromley, in greater London, it used to be known to the ancient Greeks as *Kallisté*: 'the most beautiful'.

And it is indeed a bewitching place. Snow-capped mountains and rugged granite hills, complete with perilously perched terracotta-roofed villages, sweep down to flower-strewn meadows and pristine sandy beaches. And with the wind off the sea wafting through *le maquis* – the island's colourful, herb-scented scrub – there's a heady whiff of perfumed pepper and spice in the air.

The wines, which they've been making here since Roman times, are darn good, too. There are still red wines from Niellucciu and Sciaccarellu and still whites from Vermentinu (also known as Malvasia). There are also small pockets of Ugni Blanc, Cinsault, Grenache and Syrah and, especially in the north, Muscat, which is most usually used to make a delectable, lightly fortified sweet wine, Muscat de Cap Corse.

This gorgeous little fizz is also made from the Muscat grape, known hereabouts as Muscadellu. It's produced by the Union des Vignerons Associés du Levant, near the port of Bastia and the Cap Corse in the far north of the island.

It's fresh, fruity and semisweet with faint whispers of honey on the finish and is completely, utterly disarming. It's also barely 7.5%vol and absolutely spot-on with strawberries and cream (especially after having marinated said berries in a glassful of this very wine) or simply quaffed on its own on a late summer's evening with one's loved one by one's side.

WWW.CORSICANWINES.COM

VEUVE CLICQUOT BRUT ROSÉ NV

CHAMPAGNE, FRANCE

Veuve Clicquot is one the great champagnes, no question. The Brut NV with its distinctive yellow label and packaging is known and admired the world over and when you order a bottle of 'The Widow' you know you are in for a treat.

Although the company's archives suggest that Veuve Clicquot was the first house to market vintage champagnes in 1810, it's the non-vintage wines that are the most important to it, accounting for around 95 per cent of sales. Veuve Clicquot's NV is blended every year from around 500 different wines drawn from three different grape varieties, five or six different vintages of reserve wines and hundreds of different vineyard sites and villages. The permutations are almost endless, and it takes great skill to get it so right that every time a customer buys a bottle it tastes the same. Happily, in Dominique Demarville, the company boasts an exceptional chef de cave.

The blend used for the Brut Rosé NV is similar to that used for the Yellow Label Brut NV – that is to say, with Pinot Noir taking the lion's share, then up to 30 per cent Chardonnay and up to 20 per cent Pinot Meunier. As you know, the juice of red grapes is white, and the traditional method for making rosé wine is to let the juice sit on the crushed grape skins for just a little while so as to impart only the faintest of colours. Red wine, of course, spends much longer on the skins and is therefore, well, red. Champagne, though, permits red wine to be mixed with white wine to make pink wine, and at Veuve Clicquot a hearty splash (about 12 per cent of the final blend) is added to the up-till-now white wine to give it its glorious copper/orange/pink hue.

It's wonderful stuff – my favourite pink champagne for sure – with weight and character and heady and enticing aromas of ripe wild strawberries and dried and candied fruits. It's almost too big to work as an apéritif and I prefer it with starters of smoked salmon or trout or with grilled tuna steak or even sushi.

WWW.VEUVE-CLICQUOT.COM

VEUVE CLICQUOT

LE TANGO DE LA COUPE

VILLA SANDI OPERE SERENISSIMA SPUMANTE CLASSICO DOC NV

VENETO, ITALY

The offices of Villa Sandi, owned by the Moretti Polgato family, are housed within a striking early seventeenth-century Palladian-style villa in Crocetta del Montello at the foot of the Treviso hills in Veneto, northeast Italy. It's said that Napoléon spent the night here during his Italian campaign. It's just the kind of gorgeous, white-pillared, statue-laden, stuccoed pile that features in my lottery-inspired dreams. Sadly, my boat has shown no signs of wanting to come in and I don't quite have the dosh the Moretti Polgatos do.

Mario of that ilk studied oenology and used to run the family wine estates, until he came up with the canny idea of making running shoes non-sweaty by means of a breathable rubber shoe sole. It's said that this brainwave came to him while out running in the heat of Nevada and that, troubled by his sweaty feet, he punched some holes in the soles of his shoes with a Swiss Army knife. More than happy with the result, he set up the shoe and clothing company, Geox, in 1995, and is now the thirteenth-richest man in Italy (worth a cool $1.85 billion at the time of writing). His brother Giancarlo now runs the family's wine estates.

The Moretti Polgatos have made exemplary still and sparkling wines here for generations, and their Cartizze Prosecco, in particular, is – quite rightly – very highly regarded. What has recently broken the mould, though, is their Opere Serenissima, a traditional method sparkler.

The Serenissima DOC or *appellation* (which takes its name from the nickname given to nearby Venice) was only established in 2011, and the first wine to be released from it was this Villa Sandi Opere Serenissima in 2015. It promptly won the gold medal and the Best in Class at that year's Champagne and Sparkling Wine World Championships.

And it's a winner, all right. A blend of Chardonnay and Pinot Nero (aka Pinot Noir) it's delightfully aromatic, with warm bread, pastries and fresh flowers on the nose and citrus and white stone fruit on the palate. It's beautifully balanced, too, and totally refreshing. There's nothing sweaty about it at all.

WWW.VILLASANDI.IT

WESTPORT RIVERS
BLANC DE NOIRS BRUT 2007

MASSACHUSETTS, USA

I said in the introduction that every wine in this book is available in the UK. Well, I lied. Sadly, the 2007 Westport Rivers Blanc de Noirs from Massachusetts is not yet on sale here, other than via a couple of mates of the winemaker, Bill Russell, who peddle the occasional bottle from their flat in Kensington. Not that I dare give you their number. I don't want them overrun.

Nevertheless, rather in the spirit of the Barbarians Invitational Rugby XV which, by tradition, always includes one uncapped player among its team of international thoroughbreds, I include said fizz in these pages and hope you'll let me get away with it.

I first came across Bill's wines in Neptune Oyster, a tiny seafood restaurant in Boston, Mass. I was tucking into a plate of East Coast oysters and craving some ice-cold fizz to go with them when the waitress wafted some Westport Rivers in my direction. One sip and I was immediately infatuated. So much so that I hired a car to take me to the winery that very afternoon.

And so it was that I met Bill Russell. He was thrilled by how much I had enjoyed his fizz and explained that since they had ideal glacial outwash soil and a pleasant, Gulf Stream-affected climate, there was every opportunity to make great sparkling wines as well as still Rieslings, Chardonnays and Pinot Noirs. He admitted, though, that having cracked how to make fine wines, his biggest problem was to get the Bostonians to drink them. They preferred to drink French rather than local wine.

I tasted Westport's range and was hugely impressed, the Blanc de Noirs being the standout wine. Made in the traditional method from Pinot Noir and Pinot Meunier, it's the palest of pale pinks and full of briary and almost tropical ripe fruit, with touches of brioche and toast, a fine underlying acidity and a firm, dry finish.

I hoovered it up and, having snuck a couple of bottles home, found it passed the acid test of tasting just as good on a rainy day in Brighton as it had on a scorching one in Massachusetts.

I trust some enlightened British merchant will stock it soon.

WWW.WESTPORTRIVERS.COM

MY
CHAMPAGNE
COCKTAIL
TOP TEN

THERE IS JUST SOMETHING ABOUT A CHAMPAGNE COCKTAIL.

It immediately suggests delicious decadence and the prospect of a cracking evening or – even better – afternoon ahead, full of adventure.

With some fine fizz in the mix, the cocktail will be effervescent and uplifting and rarely too savagely alcoholic (beware Ernest Hemingway's signature Death in the Afternoon, though, an unholy alliance of champagne and absinthe and nothing but). And unlike the chemical cosh of, say, an Aunt Roberta (don't ask), Sazerac, bone-dry Martini (aka Pass the Bottle) or even the sublime Negroni, you will be able to have two, maybe three, before heading off relatively unscathed.

When creating a cocktail that requires champagne or sparkling wine, remember that champagne is fuller, richer and more demanding than, for instance, Prosecco and can occasionally be too heavy and overwhelming as a mixer. Prosecco, being lighter in both alcohol and bubbles, can, in some cases, work better. Indeed, there are some cocktails that insist upon one and some that insist upon the other. And there are those in which either would do. In which case, judge for yourself.

And as with cooking, a fine cocktail relies on the best ingredients. Try not to cut corners. Don't forget that for a cocktail where a fruit juice is required, freshly squeezed or pulped juices are best. If time spent halving and squeezing several oranges is likely to spoil the moment or you really can't be bothered, invest in some bottles of freshly squeezed orange juice and some packs of Funkin fruit purées; they really are the genuine article (albeit often with added sugar) and utterly delicious, used by the world's best mixologists.

Some cocktails need the best-available fizz, be it champagne, fine sparkling or top Prosecco; many don't. But that doesn't mean you can get away with using the worst. Dirt-cheap, poor-quality Cava, for example, is still dirt-cheap, poor-quality Cava whether or not you drown it in fruit juices, fruit schnapps, brandy or whatever. Be kind to yourself and your guests and use the best you can.

BELLINI

The Bellini is one of the most decadent and satisfying of sparkling wine cocktails and, drunk in the right company and in the right place, there's nothing to touch it. It really must be made with Prosecco, the lightness and delicacy of which suits the accompanying peach nectar or purée just so.

Invented by the owner of Harry's Bar in Venice in the early 1940s, it's wonderfully simple to make, so long as you have some peaches within reach. And they should be fresh white peaches at that. I don't know anyone who can be bothered to purée their own (although a first-rate bar should), so I make sure that I always have a great big sachet of Funkin white peach purée at hand. It's very reasonably priced given that it's 90 per cent white peach and 10 per cent sugar. The bag will stay fresh in the fridge for about a week after opening.

50ml (2fl oz) peach purée
  (homemade or Funkin)
100ml (3½fl oz) Prosecco
Dash of peach schnapps
  (optional)

The classic Bellini recipe requires a champagne flute, into which you pour the peach purée, followed by the Prosecco and give it a gentle stir. Simple as. I like to add a hearty dash of peach schnapps in between the purée and the Prosecco, just to give it a bit more oomph.

'I DRINK TO MAKE OTHER PEOPLE MORE INTERESTING.'

ERNEST HEMINGWAY

JO JO

This is a strawberry version of the Bellini. I first came across it in the Hotel Danieli in Venice, where it's known as a Bucintoro (the name given to the state barge of Venice's ruling *doges*), and it's utterly scrumptious. Make it in exactly the same way you would a Bellini.

50ml (2fl oz) strawberry purée (homemade or Funkin)
Dash of strawberry schnapps (optional)
100ml (3½fl oz) Prosecco

Pour the strawberry purée into a champagne flute. Add a dash of strawberry schnapps if you fancy but don't if you don't. Top up with Prosecco and give it a slight stir.

CHAMPAGNE COCKTAIL

The Champagne Cocktail is an absolute classic and one of those reliable standby cocktails that's almost impossible to mess up, so long as you use first-rate ingredients. As the name suggests, you really should use champagne or a very fine traditional method sparkler at the very least. Prosecco and Cava won't do. And don't go lobbing in some cheap cooking brandy. It doesn't have to be Rémy Martin Louis XIII Cognac, but use the best you've got, within reason; otherwise the drink will taste bitter and off-balance.

1 white sugar cube
2 dashes of Angostura bitters
10–20ml (2–4 tsp) decent cognac
90ml (3fl oz) champagne or fine sparkling wine

Place the sugar cube in the bottom of a champagne flute. Splash it with Angostura bitters. Add the cognac and then top up with well-chilled champagne. You can lob in a maraschino cherry if you insist, but I prefer it as it comes.

FRENCH 75

The classic French 75 was invented during the First World War by one Harry MacElhone of the New York Bar in Paris, and the cocktail was so-named because the kick it gave was said to be similar to the sensation of being pounded by the French 75mm field gun. Not only is it delicious, it's deliciously simple to make, comprising just champagne, gin and fresh lemon juice.

At Brighton Gin (in which I must declare an interest, being one of the co-founders), we gave this classic a bit of a twist, calling it the Sussex 75. The only difference is that we insist on using Brighton Gin (natch), plus a fine Sussex sparkler such as Ridgeview, Breaky Bottom or Ambriel.

25ml (1fl oz) gin
25ml (1fl oz) freshly squeezed
   lemon juice
10ml (2 tsp) sugar syrup
   (Monin Gomme syrup for
   choice)
Champagne/sparkling wine

Pour the gin, lemon juice and syrup into a champagne flute and stir. Top up with champagne (for a French 75) or a fine Sussex sparkler (for a Sussex 75) and garnish with a twist of lemon.

'A MAN'S GOT TO BELIEVE IN SOMETHING. I BELIEVE I'LL HAVE ANOTHER DRINK.'

W.C. FIELDS

BUCK'S FIZZ AND MIMOSA

The classic Buck's Fizz was invented just up the road from Brooks's (see page 163) in Buck's Club, Mayfair, in 1921, allegedly to give the idle members with time on their hands an excuse to drink somewhat earlier in the morning than was hitherto usual. It comprises two parts champagne – or decent sparkling wine – to one part fresh orange juice (NOT carton orange juice).

Just to be pedantic, if you change the ingredients and measurements slightly to half Prosecco and half orange juice, you get a Mimosa. Both the Buck's Fizz and Mimosa are perfect mid-morning fare: fresh, fruity, zesty, light in alcohol and crammed with vitamins.

⅓ part fresh orange juice
  for Buck's Fizz
  (or ½ for Mimosa)
⅔ part champagne for
  Buck's Fizz (or ½ Prosecco
  for Mimosa)

Fill a champagne flute with the required amount of fresh orange juice and top up with champagne or Prosecco.

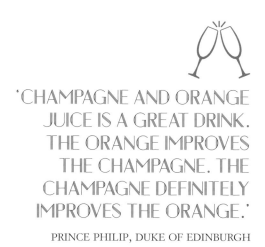

'CHAMPAGNE AND ORANGE JUICE IS A GREAT DRINK. THE ORANGE IMPROVES THE CHAMPAGNE. THE CHAMPAGNE DEFINITELY IMPROVES THE ORANGE.'

PRINCE PHILIP, DUKE OF EDINBURGH

KIR ROYAL

Kir is a simple drink – it hardly merits the term 'cocktail' – comprising dry white wine and crème de cassis. It was invented by Canon Félix Kir, a French Resistance fighter during the Second World War, and, after hostilities ended, mayor of Dijon.

The local Bourgogne Aligoté white wine was – and often still is – almost unpalatably sharp, acidic and dry. To alleviate this, Canon Kir was in the habit of adding a sweetening dash of crème de cassis. This caught on and the drink was named after him. A Kir Royal simply substitutes champagne or fine French fizz for the still white wine and is a delightful drink, best served well chilled while sitting on some sun-drenched terrace around 6P.M.

10ml (2 tsp) crème de cassis
90ml (3fl oz) champagne or
   fine French fizz

Pour the cassis into the bottom of a champagne flute. Top up with champagne. Some folk like to stir it slightly to blend the two ingredients; others like to let the cassis sit at the bottom of the glass, enjoying the increasing sweetness and blackcurrant-ness as they near the end of the drink.

SBAGLIATO

Sbagliato is the Italian word for 'mistake' and this is a mistaken Negroni, invented, created or stumbled upon in Bar Basso in Milan. It's said that in the busy hubbub of the bar, a customer's request for a Negroni (that classic cocktail made from equal parts of Campari, sweet red vermouth and gin) was misheard by the barman who, for some reason, substituted Prosecco for the gin. The customer liked it so much that he had another; his friends joined him in doing likewise, and thus a new cocktail was born.

30ml (1fl oz) sweet red
 vermouth
30ml (1fl oz) Campari
Ice (optional)
30ml (1fl oz) Prosecco
Twist or slice of orange
 (optional)

Some people serve this in a champagne flute, others (I think more properly) in a whisky tumbler over ice. As for proportions, make it as you would a Negroni. Pour the vermouth and the Campari over ice in said tumbler. Top up with Prosecco and garnish with a twist or slice of orange.

'MEET ME DOWN IN THE BAR! WE'LL DRINK BREAKFAST TOGETHER.'

W.C. FIELDS, *THE BIG BROADCAST OF 1938*

APEROL SPRITZ

The Aperol Spritz must surely be the most popular *aperitivo* in Italy, and it is indeed a beauty: zesty and refreshing with a touch of bitterness and a hint of orange sweetness. I reckon it's pretty much the finest of light summer drinks.

Aperol is produced by Campari and is quite similar to it, although markedly less bitter. It's also a rather alarming neon orange in colour whereas Campari is a pleasing deep maroon. Nevertheless, Aperol makes an unparalleled spritz.

75ml (2½fl oz) Prosecco
50ml (2fl oz) Aperol
25ml (1fl oz) soda water
Slice of orange

Put plenty of ice into a large wine glass. Pour in the Prosecco, wait for a second or two for the froth to die down, then add the Aperol and swirl the glass. Top up with the soda water and a slice of orange. Don't be too fussed by the proportions; they're only a guideline, so mix it to taste. An Aperol Spritz is hard to get wrong and impossible not to enjoy.

'YOU'RE NOT DRUNK IF YOU
CAN LIE ON THE FLOOR
WITHOUT HOLDING ON.'

DEAN MARTIN

BLACK VELVET

Invented by the barman at Brooks's Club in St James's Street in 1861 for members mourning the death of Prince Albert, a Black Velvet is simply Guinness and champagne, half and half, ideally served in a pint pewter tankard or, if you're taking things easy and can't cope with a grown-up portion, a champagne flute. It's an outrageous combination, Guinness and champagne, and has no business working at all, but it's ridiculously delicious and perfect alongside an 11A.M. plate of oysters.

You need draught or bottled draught Guinness and a fine champagne that's not too dry, so don't use a brut zéro or such like. Bollinger Special Cuvée Brut NV, Pol Roger Brut NV or Veuve Clicquot Brut NV would be my choice. And cheapskates, please note: Cava will NOT do.

½ pint Guinness
½ pint champagne

Half-fill the tankard (or champagne flute if you insist) with Guinness, then top up slowly with champagne. Take your time pouring, as the drink can froth over quite easily. And take your time drinking, as it's a beverage to savour.

BOURBON LANCER

This is quite a punchy cocktail and surprisingly delicious, mixing as it does champagne and bourbon. And when I say champagne, you can in fact use any fine sparkling wine, although it's best to use a traditional method fizz rather than Prosecco or similar, which I find too light and just a tad too sweet for this.

45ml (1¾fl oz) Bourbon
80ml (3 fl oz) champagne
3 dashes of Angostura bitters
Ice
Twist of lemon

Fill a highball glass with ice. Pour in the Bourbon, then the champagne. Stir gently, but not so much as to reduce the sparkle. Garnish with a twist of lemon.

GLOSSARY OF WINE TERMS

Assemblage (French): The blend of wines that goes to make the final fizz.

Blanc de Blancs (French): A white wine made solely from white grapes.

Blanc de Noirs (French): A white wine made solely from red grapes.

Bodega (Spanish): A cellar or winery.

Bottle Age: The period between bottling and consumption.

Brut (French): Dry.

Brut Extra (French): Dry to very dry.

Brut Nature, Brut Sauvage, Brut Zéro (French): Very dry.

Cartizze (Italian): The finest level of Prosecco, named after the hill on which the best quality grapes are grown.

Cava (Spanish): The traditional method fizz of Spain (mainly from the Penedès).

Cave (French): Cellar.

Cépage (French): The term for grape variety.

Chai (French): Cellar.

Champagne Method: See Traditional Method.

Charmat Process: The method by which many sparkling wines such as Prosecco are made.

Chef de Cave (French): Technically, the cellarmaster but in fact the winemaker.

Crémant (French): The term given to French (and Luxembourgish) sparkling wines made outside Champagne using the traditional method.

Cuve Close (French): Another name for the Charmat Process.

Cuvée (French): A particular blend or wine.

Dégorgement/Disgorgement: The removal of the sediment from a bottle after its secondary fermentation.

Demi-Sec (French): Medium sweet to sweet.

Dolce (Italian): Sweet.

Dosage (French): The addition of a wine/sugar solution (the *liqueur d'expédition*) immediately before a traditional method sparkler is bottled.

Doux (French): Sweet to very sweet.

Extra Dry/Extra Sec: Dry to medium dry.

Fermentation: Process whereby yeasts convert sugar into alcohol and thus grape juice into wine.

Finish: The aftertaste of any given wine.

Franciacorta: An Italian sparkler which, alone with champagne, shares its name with its region, its wine and its method of production.

Frizzante (Italian): Sparkling.

Grand Cru (French): Term given to the finest vineyards in Champagne.

Grande Marque (French): A no-longer-official term used in Champagne for the grandest producers.

Horizontal tasting: A tasting of several wines from the same vintage but different producers.

Lees: The sediment left behind after fermentation.

Length: The length of time the taste remains in the mouth after swallowing or spitting out a wine.

CONTINUED OVERLEAF

Liqueur de tirage (French): The wine/yeast/sugar solution added to Champagne Method wines to encourage the secondary fermentation.

Liqueur d'expédition (French): The wine/sugar solution added to traditional method wines during the dosage.

Maceration: The period during vinification in which the fermenting grape juice is in contact with the skins and the pips.

Méthode Champenoise: See Traditional Method.

Méthode Traditionelle: See Traditional Method.

Mousse: The effervescence in the glass as a sparkling wine is poured.

Mousseux (French): Sparkling.

Non-vintage (NV): A blend of wines from more than one vintage.

Pétillant (French): Slightly sparkling.

Punt: The indentation at the base of a wine bottle which catches any sediment and strengthens the glass.

Récolte (French): Crop or vintage.

Remuage (French): The regular turning of traditional method bottles in order to trap their sediment prior to their disgorgement, also known as 'riddling'.

Reserve wines: Wines from previous vintages used alongside the current vintage to blend non-vintage wines, thus ensuring consistency of house style.

Riddling: See above.

Sec (French): Literally 'dry' but in fact medium to medium sweet.

Sekt (German): Sparkling wine.

Spumante (Italian): Sparkling.

Sur Lattes (French): The practice of maturing champagne/sparkling wine bottles on their sides.

Tank Method: Another name for the Charmat method.

Traditional Method: (also known as **Méthode Champenoise**, **Méthode Traditionelle** or **Champagne Method**): The method of making the finest sparkling wines – with its secondary fermentation in bottle – as practised in Champagne and other top regions.

Transfer Method: A way of making wines sparkle that's similar to – but less complicated and less admirable – than the traditional method.

Vendange (French): Harvest.

Vertical Tasting: A tasting of several wines from the same producer but in different vintages.

Vigneron (French): Winemaker.

Vinification: Winemaking.

Viticulture: Cultivation of grapes.

WHERE TO BUY
FINE FIZZ

UK

YAPP BROTHERS
The Old Brewery
Water Street, Mere
Wiltshire BA12 6DY
www.yapp.co.uk

BERRY BROS & RUDD
3 St. James's Street
London SW1A 1EG
www.bbr.com

TANNERS
26 Wyle Cop
Shrewsbury
Shropshire SY1 1XD
www.tanners-wines.co.uk

PRIVATE CELLAR
57 High Street
Wicken
Cambridgeshire CB7 5XR
www.privatecellar.co.uk

FROM VINEYARDS DIRECT
www.fromvineyardsdirect.co.uk

CORNEY & BARROW
1 Thomas More Street
London E1W 1YZ

8 Academy Street
Ayr
Ayrshire KA7 1HT
www.corneyandbarrow.com

LEA & SANDEMAN
170 Fulham Road
London SW10 9PR
www.leaandsandeman.co.uk

SWIG
188 Sutton Court Road
London W4 3HR
www.swig.co.uk

THE CHAMPAGNE COMPANY
www.thechampagnecompany.com

QUAFF
139 Portland Road
Hove
East Sussex BN3 5QJ
www.quaffwine.com

D. BYRNE & CO
Victoria Buildings
12 King Street
Clitheroe
Lancashire BB7 2EP
www.dbyrne-finewines.co.uk

RED SQUIRREL
The Acton Business Centre Y14
School Road
London NW10 6TD
www.redsquirrelwine.com

JUSTERINI & BROOKS
61 St. James's Street
London SW1A 1LZ

14 Alva Street
Edinburgh EH2 4QG
www.justerinis.com

CHAMPAGNE DIRECT
www.champagnedirect.co.uk

MARKS & SPENCER
www.marksandspencer.com

WAITROSE
www.waitrose.com

MAJESTIC
www.majestic.co.uk

TESCO
www.tesco.com

SAINSBURY'S
www.sainsburys.co.uk

THE CO-OPERATIVE
www.co-operativefood.co.uk

AUSTRALIA

PRINCE WINE STORE
166 Bank Street
South Melbourne 3205

40 Hansard Street
Zetland 2017

80 Primrose Street
Essendon 3181
www.princewinestore.com.au

EAST END CELLARS
25 Vardon Avenue
Adelaide 5000
www.eastendcellars.com.au

CHAMPAGNE GALLERY
www.champagnegallery.com.au

DAN MURPHY'S
www.danmurphys.com.au

FIRST CHOICE LIQUOR
www.firstchoiceliquor.com.au

VINTAGE CELLARS
www.vintagecellars.com.au

NEW ZEALAND

WINE DIRECT
www.winedirect.co.nz

WINENZ
www.winenz.com

USA

NEIGHBORHOOD CELLAR
246 W Davis Street
Dallas, TX
www.neighborhoodcellar.com

BEVMO!
www.bevmo.com

COST PLUS WORLD MARKET
www.worldmarket.com

K&L WINE MERCHANTS
www.klwines.com

WINE.COM
www.wine.com

TRADER JOE'S
www.traderjoes.com

WHOLE FOODS
www.wholefoodsmarket.com

CANADA

BC LIQUOR STORES
www.bcliquorstores.com

INDEX

When a wine name consists of a first name and surname the order is dictated by the surname. The denominations 'Cave de', 'Domaine (de)', 'Castello' etc. are ignored for the purposes of alphabetization

PUBLISHING DIRECTOR Sarah Lavelle
CREATIVE DIRECTOR Helen Lewis
COMMISSIONING EDITOR Céline Hughes
COVER DESIGNER Nicola Ellis
BOOK DESIGNER Gemma Hayden
PICTURE RESEARCHER Liz Boyd
PRODUCTION CONTROLLER Tom Moore
PRODUCTION DIRECTOR Vincent Smith

First published in 2017 by
Quadrille Publishing Limited
Pentagon House
52–54 Southwark Street
London SE1 1UN
www.quadrille.com

Quadrille is an imprint of
Hardie Grant
www.hardiegrant.com

Text © 2017 Jonathan Ray
Design and layout © 2017 Quadrille
Publishing Limited

Cataloguing in Publication Data:
A catalogue record for this book is
available from the British Library.

ISBN 978 178713 079 1

Printed and bound in China

PICTURE CREDITS

p.2 Original Champagne Bollinger label from the 1850s, Champagne Bollinger;
p.25 Art Deco Champagne Ayala poster, Champagne Ayala; p.34 Retrograph/
Mary Evans Picture Library; p.67 Lordprice Collection/Alamy Stock Photo;
p.105 Retrograph/Mary Evans Picture Library; p.133 Shawshots/Alamy Stock
Photo; p.143 L'Instant Taittinger, c.1984 (colour litho), French School, (20th
century)/Private Collection/Bridgeman Images; p.149 Advertising champagne
for Veuve Clicquot Champagne designed by Georges Goursat aka SEM, Maison
Veuve Clicquot archives; p.155 Lordprice Collection/Alamy Stock Photo; p.161
Poster advertising Campari Bitter, 1948 (colour litho), Fisa (fl. 1948) /Private
Collection/DaTo Images/Bridgeman Images

ACKNOWLEDGEMENTS

As you might imagine, this volume has been a hugely enjoyable to research. It was made all the more so by the kind assistance I received from the many producers and their representatives included in these pages, sadly far too numerous to thank by name here.

I would like to thank Céline Hughes and Sarah Lavelle for coming up with the idea in the first place and for asking me to undertake it, and to thank Céline for her remarkably efficient and patient editing. Thank you, too, to Nicola Ellis for the delightful cover and to Gemma Hayden for making the pages inside look so beautiful.

John Franklin, Nicky Smith, Kate Sweet and Emma Wellings have also been especially helpful and generous with their advice regarding the wines.

Needless to say, any mistakes that remain in these pages are down to my own ineptitude and slackness and nobody else's.

Finally, huge thanks to my wife, Marina, whose readiness to open another bottle and help with research knew no bounds.

'WRITE DRUNK;
EDIT SOBER.'

ERNEST HEMINGWAY